# THE ROYAL NAVY AT DEVONPORT SINCE 1900

## by Lt Cdr Ben Warlow RN

The Torpedo Training Ship(s) *Defiance* originally lay in the River Lynher, but in 1931 the 'establishment' moved to Wilcove. By then it comprised the cruiser *Andromeda*, frigate *Inconstant* and cruiser/depot ship *Vulcan*. They remained there until they were paid off on 14 July 1954. The establishment continued ashore at Wilcove until 20 April 1959, when it was absorbed into the RN Barracks, *HMS Drake*. *Vulcan* (*Defiance III*) was towed away to the breakers in December 1955, *Inconstant* (*Defiance II*) in April 1956 and *Andromeda* (*Defiance*) in August 1956. In the background can be seen a Fort class Armament Store Ship lying off the RN Armament Depot at Bull Point, while the battleship *Howe* lies in reserve in the left background.

*(Author's Collection)*

# The Royal Navy at Devonport since 1900

Devonport, called Plymouth Dock until 1824, was known throughout the Navy as 'Guz'. It was from here that Drake sailed to defeat the Spanish Armada. The 20th Century would continue the great tradition of Drake, Raleigh, Hawkins and Grenville. The waters where the estuaries of the Rivers Plym and Tamar met - called Plymouth Sound - had been made safer by the construction of a 1700-yard long breakwater, completed in 1848. These sheltered waters, watched over by Plymouth Hoe, were the arrival and departure points for many voyages, but the main Naval activity was based on the River Tamar and the adjacent land on both its Cornish and the Devon banks. At the turn of the century, many of the sailors in port were housed in wooden walls, with the *Impregnable* group as Flagship and training ship. The *Lion* and *Implacable* were boys' training ships, but both would depart before the Great War. *Defiance* was the torpedo school, where the earliest wireless experiments had been carried out. *Cambridge* was the gunnery school. The *Indus* (4 ships) was a mechanical training establishment and workshop. Engineer Officers were trained at Keyham. The Royal Naval Hospital at Stonehouse had been opened in 1762, and the Royal William Yard, the store for victualling, in 1835. In 1890 the main naval depot had moved into the new barracks (*Vivid*) from the hulk *RoyalAdelaide*. *Vivid* became known as 'Jago's Mansions', after the Catering Officer who introduced great improvements to the dining facilities for the men. The new barracks bordered on the northern end of the Dockyard, where ships were built and refitted. The Dockyard was to build many ships, battleships, cruisers, sloops, and even an aircraft carrier, for the Navy in the 20th Century.

1900 was a time of great change for the Navy, with the introduction of turbine driven ships, torpedo boat destroyers, aircraft and submarines, and the Royal Dockyard also expanded to meet the new, technical commitments. The gunnery school moved into the Barracks in 1907, but the name *Cambridge* was to return to the area in 1956 when taken up for the Gunnery range at Wembury, just outside Plymouth Sound. With the advent of the Great War, Devonport also saw the arrival of the Royal Naval Air Service, based on the Cattewater and Mount Batten, and with a Kite Balloon Station across the River Tamar at Merifield. Another Boys' Training Ship (*Powerful*) was commissioned in 1913 in three hulks, and finally merged with *Impregnable* in 1919. During the Great War, Devonport was also one of the major Auxiliary Patrol bases.

Between the wars, the Torpedo School *Defiance*, by then comprising four steel hulks and with the old wooden wall gone, had shifted berth from the River Lynher to Wilcove, on the Cornish side of the Tamar. At about that time the *Impregnable* paid off, though the establishment was commissioned on shore from 1935 to 1948. In 1934 the Barracks name was changed from *Vivid* to *Drake*.

War came early to Devonport, when the survivors from the torpedoed aircraft carrier *Courageous* were brought ashore in September 1939. Another early loss from the Port Division was the battleship *Royal Oak* (built at Devonport 1914-16). A more cheering event was the return of the battle-scarred cruiser *Exeter* in February 1940 after her gallant action in the South Atlantic. Further tragedies were to strike the Port Division, with major losses

of life in the sinkings of the carrier *Glorious* off Norway, the cruiser *Gloucester* off Crete, and the battle-cruiser *Repulse* and battleship *Prince of Wales* off Malaya. The Honours Board in *Drake* Drill Shed lists the many Devonport ships that were lost. Meanwhile, the city of Plymouth underwent one of the severest blitzes that Britain suffered. During the war many ships were to return to Devonport for repairs to their battle damage. New training establishments were set up on the Cornish side of the river, *Raleigh* for RN Special Reservists with an Artificer Training Establishment, later named *Fisgard*, alongside it. With the war being taken to the enemy, the banks of the River Tamar became covered with American troops preparing for the Normandy landings. Meanwhile, cruisers and destroyers based on the port swept the Bay of Biscay and Channel for blockade-runners and enemy warships operating form the French ports. A Coastal Forces' Base (*Black Bat*) was established at 13 wharf in 1943.

With the ending of the war, the safe waters of the Tamar, and River Lynher were soon filled with ships in reserve, destroyers and frigates lying four deep in long trots stretching north beyond Brunel's Royal Albert bridge. There were other, larger ships too, including the battleship *Howe* and aircraft carrier *Unicorn*. The Reserve Fleet was named *Orion* in 1950, after one of the port's most famous cruisers of the war. At Turnchapel the Boom Defence Establishment *Ubiquity* was commissioned from 1947-48, and then became a civil establishment. The Royal Naval Engineering College had begun its move from Keyham to Manadon in 1940, and was named *Thunderer* in 1946. The ex-liner *Alaunia* was moored in the river as a training ship for engine room ratings from 1947 to 1956.

In 1949 the streets of Devonport and Plymouth rang to cheers as the crew of the frigate *Amethyst* marched through the city after their return from their dash down the Yangtse River. In 1956 there was a stir again as ships, loaded with troops and material, sailed for Suez.

In 1954 the Torpedo School (*Defiance*) paid off and the staff moved into the Barracks, where the training continued until April 1959. However, the name returned to Devonport in 1972, when the depot ship *Forth* was renamed and employed as a Fleet Maintenance Base and depot ship for the Second Submarine Squadron. A Hydrographic School had been established in *Drake* and worked alongside the survey ships based on Devonport.

As the Navy modernised and developed, nuclear submarines became based on the port, and special facilities for their refits were built. Large covered docks were opened in September 1977 for refitting frigates, and new jetties completed in place of the old coaling wharf at the north end of the dockyard. In April 1978 the depot ship *Defiance* paid off, and the facility re-provided in new buildings ashore. These were commissioned as *Defiance* from 1981 to 1994. A new complex for ships to berth and maintain with the help of the Fleet Maintenance Base was completed at Weston Mill Lake, with easy access to the Barracks.

In 1982 Devonport was again preparing ships for war, as a Task Force was prepared to retake the Falkland Islands. Merchant ships taken up from trade were fitted with flight decks, and long hours were worked preparing and storing these vessels prior to their sailing. There were cheers too, when the ships returned victorious, though the Devonport frigates *Ardent* and *Antelope* and the container ship *Atlantic Conveyor* failed to return, having been lost in the endeavour.

In 1983 the Artificer Training Establishment *Fisgard* closed. The Royal Naval Engineering College and the Royal Naval Hospital both closed in 1995. Meanwhile, on 14 April 1989 the Type 22 frigate *Cumberland* with the Commander-in-Chief Fleet embarked became the first ship to go alongside the new Weston Mill Lake Jetty to the north of the Naval Base. With the closure of the Portland Naval Base in 1995, the work up staff moved to Devonport, and today the harbour is busy with ships of many nations taking advantage of this unique facility.

Towards the end of the 20th century, the services became more involved in peace keeping operations, and troops were required in distant countries. These operations have required the Navy to concentrate on its Amphibious Warfare Capability, and Devonport has become a "centre for Amphibious Excellence."

Meanwhile, the new deterrent submarines - the Vanguard class, have been introduced into service, and the docks and facilities at Devonport were modified to permit the refitting of these 16,000 ton leviathans. The first refit (of *Vanguard*) took place between 2002 and 2004, and *Victorious* arrived for the second of these refits in early 2005.

There has been much change for the Navy and the Dockyard since 1900. It has been full of strife at times, but during that period the best traditions of the port and the region have been maintained. I am proud to have been present and shared that experience, and hope that my children and grandchildren will see it continued through the 21st Century. May the traditional Port Division cry of 'Oggie, Oggie, Oggie!' continue to echo down through the ages.

My thanks are due to Andy Endacott and Dave Scoble for their work on the initial picture compilation, and also to Syd Goodman who has kindly permitted the use of some of his historic collection.

Ben Warlow
2005

The *Impregnable* had been at Devonport since 1828 as a training ship, and later also as the Flagship. By the turn of the century the original ship had been replaced by the *Howe* of 1860, and had been joined by the frigate *Inconstant* and fifth rate *Circe*. The ironclad *Black Prince* joined the group in 1910. The cruiser *Powerful* joined in 1919 - having been a training ship at Devonport from 1913 with the cruiser *Andromeda*, which became *Impregnable II*, and corvette *Caroline* (which became *Impregnable IV*). *Impregnable* paid off in 1929, the last boys being drafted on 1 January 1919. The hulls were then either sold or incorporated into the *Defiance* establishment. Thus some of these hulls served long periods in Devonport under various names, giving valuable, if not seagoing, service. The name *Impregnable* was used for a training establishment on shore at St. Budeaux from 1935, and post-war for an overflow accommodation camp.

*(S.V. Goodman Collection)*

The Second Rate *Lion* of 1847 became a boys' training ship at Devonport in 1871, after service on the Clyde as a coast guard vessel. She was joined by the ***Implacable*** (ex French ***Duguay-Trouin***). Both ships are seen here lying off the Cornish bank of the River Tamar near Torpoint. *Lion* was sold in July 1905, the training role being absorbed by ***Impregnable***. The ***Implacable*** was lent for preservation in 1912. In World War II she was a stores ship at Portsmouth. After further use as a training ship she was scuttled in December 1949.

(*Author's Collection*)

The original **Defiance** was launched at Pembroke in March 1861 but her 91 guns were never installed. Instead, she was taken into service as the Torpedo School at Devonport, commissioning on 13 December 1884. She lay at the mouth of the River Lynher until replaced in 1931. In this view, ahead of her lies the Apollo Class cruiser **Spartan**. Launched in 1891, she joined the **Defiance** group in 1907 to provide power and for wireless instruction. Ahead of **Spartan** lies the **Flamingo**, a gun vessel used for storing, testing and working electric cables. Beyond **Defiance** can be seen the Hamoaze busy with shipping, whilst the Great Western Railway line is in the foreground. The **Defiance** sailors built their own station for the trains.

*(Author's Collection)*

A class is seen under instruction in the 1861 sloop **Perseus**, which was **Defiance II** from 1904-1907. The **Defiance's** bows can be seen in the background, the two ships being joined by a walkway. These were the early days for the use of electricity, note the rather frightened but curious observers behind the companionway! Instruction was also carried out on mines and torpedoes. Later anti-submarine training also came under **Defiance's** wing. The first radio transmissions were received onboard a ship in **Defiance**, her then Captain, Henry B Jackson, later becoming an Admiral of the Fleet and Fellow of the Royal Society. *(Author's Collection)*

This early view of the entrance to the River Tamar shows the Victualling Yard (Royal William Yard) built in 1826-35 by Sir John Rennie. In the foreground lies the Commander-in-Chief's yacht *Vivid*, ex *Capercailzie*, which became the nominal depot ship for the Barracks when they were commissioned as *Vivid* on 1 January 1890. Beyond the Victualling Yard can be seen Plymouth Sound and Stadden Heights, whilst the Creek to the left leads to the Royal Naval Hospital (completed in 1762) at Stonehouse. The Commander-in-Chief's residence had a magnificent view of all ships entering and leaving harbour from this vantage point. Underground here was built the Second World War Maritime Headquarters, which closed at the start of the 21st Century.

(*S.V. Goodman Collection*)

The pre-Dreadnought battleship **Resolution** is seen here off Torpoint, with South Yard in the background. She had been launched at Jarrow on 28 May 1892. Of 14,150 tons, she was armed with two twin 13.5-inch and ten 6-inch guns and had a speed of 18 knots. Her main armament could only be loaded in the fore and aft position. She was made obsolete by later battleships, particularly **Dreadnought**, and was broken up in Holland in 1914. Only one of her class (**Revenge**, renamed **Redoubtable**) survived to give service (as a monitor) in the Great War.

(*S.V. Goodman Collection*)

The *Queen* was a pre-Dreadnought battleship. She was laid down at Devonport in March 1901, was launched on 8 March 1902 and completed in April 1904. Of 15,000 tons, she was armed with two twin 12-inch, twelve 6-inch and sixteen 12-pounder guns, and could steam at 18 knots. She was the first battleship with stockless anchors, easing the work of the forecastle party. Although made obsolete by *Dreadnought* (1906), she served in the Great War at the Dardanelles, and from 1915-18 was the base ship at Taranto. She was sold in November 1920, her hull arriving at Preston for breaking up in August 1921.                    (*Andy Endacott Collection*)

The **King Edward VII** was the nameship of a class of pre-Dreadnought battleships of 16,350 tons known as 'the Wobbly Eight'. She was built at Devonport Dockyard, being launched on 23 July 1903 and completed on 7 February 1905. She was armed with four 12-inch, four 9.2inch, ten 6-inch and fourteen 12-pounder guns and had a speed of 18.5 knots, which she exceeded on trials. On 6 January 1916 off Cape Wrath she hit a mine (laid by the German minelayer **Moewe**) while on passage to Scapa Flow from Belfast. She was taken in tow by the collier **Melita** and destroyer **Kempenfelt** but sank later that day. Her crew was rescued by destroyers. King Edward, when he launched her, had directed she should always be a Flagship, and this was her first voyage without an Admiral onboard.

*(Andy Endacott Collection)*

11

The battleship **Trafalgar** of 11,940 tons had been launched at Portsmouth on 20 September 1887. Her completion was delayed until March 1990 awaiting her 13.5-inch guns. She managed to fire 4 rounds in nine minutes from one gun. After seven years as Flagship on the Mediterranean Station, she became guardship at Portsmouth. She entered the reserve Fleet at Devonport in 1905, and in 1907 transferred to Sheerness to be a turret and submerged torpedo-tube drill ship. She is seen her aground at the entrance to the Tamar in 1907 - presumably as she left for Sheerness. She was sold in May 1911 to G. Garnham for breaking up.

*(Andy Endacott Collection)*

Work started on Plymouth Dock in 1691, in the area known as South Yard. The North Yard (Steam Yard) development did not start till 1844. Plymouth Dock was renamed Devonport in 1824. This view of The Terrace in South Yard shows men on their way to work. The grandeur of the houses in The Terrace, originally called The Walk and comprising residences for Dockyard Officers, contrasts with the heavy labour of shipbuilding being carried out just at the foot of the slope on which the men are walking. Only two of the 13 houses in The Terrace survived the Blitz of March and April 1941.

*(S.V. Goodman Collection)*

The torpedo gunboat *Speedwell* was launched at Devonport Dockyard on 15 March 1889. Of 735 tons, she was armed with two 4.7-inch and four 3-pounder guns and also carried three torpedo tubes. She had a speed of 19 knots. She first commissioned for the Channel Squadron, was placed in reserve from 1894-99 and then became a tender to the Queensferry coast guard ship *Rodney*. She was later converted to be a minesweeper and as such served in the Great War. In 1919 she became a tender to the receiving ship *Colleen* at Queenstown before being sold in March 1920 to the Cornish Salvage Company of Ilfracombe.

*(S.V. Goodman Collection)*

The *Sentinel* (ex *Inchkeith*) was a scout cruiser of 2,940 tons launched by Vickers on 19 April 1904 and completed in April 1905. Originally armed with ten 12-pounder and eight 3-pounder guns, she was later refitted with nine 4-inch guns and one 3-inch gun. She also had 2 torpedo tubes. This view shows her on 18 May 1905 just after completion off South Yard - note the turtle back forecastle and three short funnels. She was sold in January 1923 and arrived at Sunderland to be broken up on 20 June 1923 after stranding whilst on passage.

*(S.V. Goodman Collection)*

This group of eight 'A' class submarines are lying together at Devonport. The photograph has 'Wear' written on it – probably referring to Wearde Quay where the Torpedo School *Defiance* lay at this time. The vessel in the distance appears to be an old sloop, possibly a tender to *Defiance*. All these submarines were built by Vickers and launched between 9 June 1903 (*A-4*) and 8 March 1905 (*A-11*). They were of 180 tons and 99 feet long (*A-4* was slightly smaller). They had petrol motors to drive them at 12 knots on the surface, with electric motors giving them 8 knots underwater. *A-8* sank off Plymouth breakwater while changing crews but was later salved. *A-7* was not so fortunate, and was lost on 16 January 1914 in Whitsand Bay. She became embedded in the mud and attempts to salvage her were given up on 2 March 1914. Her 11 crew were lost. *A-11* was broken up at Portsmouth in May 1920. The remaining vessels were sold for breaking up in 1919/20.

(*Steve Bush Collection*)

The second class cruiser **Spartan** of 3,600 tons was launched by Armstrong Mitchell on 25 February 1891 and was completed the next year. A sister to **Retribution**, her lack of firepower and general lack of seaworthiness led to her early paying off. However, she was taken up for harbour service. In 1907 she joined the **Defiance** training group in the River Lynher to provide power. She was renamed **Defiance II** in August 1921, and was not sold until 26 June 1931.

(*S.V. Goodman Collection*)

The Majestic class battleship *Victorious* is seen here coaling ship. Of 14,900 tons, she was launched by Chatham Dockyard on 19 October 1895 and completed in 1896. She was armed with four 12-inch and twelve 6-inch guns and was designed for 17 knots but achieved 18.7 knots on trials. At this speed she used a lot of coal, and the 'EXPRESS' coaling lighter *C80*, built for the Fleet Coaling Service by Thames Iron Works Shipbuilding & Engineering Co. of London can be seen alongside her. *Victorious* was disarmed in 1915, her 12-inch guns being used by Lord Clive class monitors, and she became a base for dockyard workers at Scapa Flow from 1916-19, later being renamed *Indus II*. She was sold in 1922 and re-sold in 1923 for breaking up.

(*Steve Bush Collection*)

This scene shows the dirt, grime, and heavy labour required to replenish the coal bunkers of a ship. Coal is being shovelled into sacks, which were then swung inboard and emptied into the ship's bunkers. Both men and the ship became covered with coal dust and clearing up was a big task. It was not until furnace fuel oil was introduced with the Queen Elizabeth class battleships early in the Great War that this task started to disappear, but coal fired battleships served till the late 1920s, and there were still coal fired ships in the 1960s. The introduction of furnace fuel oil was delayed because of the fear of ships having to operate in areas where stocks were not available. (*Andy Endacott Collection*)

In 1854-56 a tunnel was built to link the South and North Yards in Devonport. Originally it was for pedestrians and horses and carts, but later a railway line, connected to the national network, was laid through it. The line opened in August 1867 and was broad gauge. A third rail was laid in 1876, and in 1892 it became standard gauge. This waggon had compartments for the Admiral Superintendent and Principal Officers, another for senior officers and a third for subordinate officers. A second covered waggon had compartments for chargemen and senior ratings, and three other waggons were for others using the half-hourly service. A proper station was built at the Barracks, and allowed ship's companies going on draft to be embarked direct into their train for their journey to the port where the ship they were to commission lay. Diesel engines were introduced in 1956, a few years before the passenger line closed. A flyover between yards was opened in 1963 allowing vehicles to go between yards without leaving the base, and the last passenger train ran on 16 May 1966. *(S.V. Goodman Collection)*

The dockyard tug **Pert** was built at Southampton by Thornycroft and was completed in 1916. She had two independent paddle wheels and blades that could be feathered. She was of 1,023 tons, and the largest tug then in Admiralty service. She had a speed of 13 knots. The colour of the band around her funnel indicated the department of the dockyard to which she was attached: blue for Captain of the Dockyard, red for the Armament depot and green for the Victualling Yard. She took part in the 1953 Coronation Review at Spithead. Withdrawn from service in October 1961, she was sold for breaking up in Holland in June 1962.

*(S.V. Goodman Collection)*

Dockyard workers are seen streaming out of the main gate to the South part of the dockyard, passing the Royal Sailors' Rest, which was conveniently sited ready to provide some comfort for the sailors in the ships in the Dockyard. This gate - the Fore Street Gate - was incorporated into the Yard after the war when the Yard was extended into the area of Fore Street flattened during the Blitz of 1941. On the pillar to the left of the gate was mounted the Yard's Call Bell, cast in 1859, and which announced the start and end of work. It was provided with a cover in 1877.

*(S.V. Goodman Collection)*

The battleship *Orion* was launched at Portsmouth Dockyard on 20 August 1910 and completed in 1912. Of 22,500 tons she was armed with five twin 13.5-inch and sixteen 4-inch guns. The 13.5-inch guns were new, and these were the first battleships with all their big guns on the centre-line. She carried out trials with her sister ship *Thunderer* to evaluate the use of the director system in gunnery. *Orion* had been selected as she had the best practice results in 13.5-inch firings, while *Thunderer* used director control. As a result directors came into general use. *Orion* was sold in December 1922 and is seen here leaving Devonport, with the Royal William Yard in the background, under tow for breaking up at Queenborough in February 1923.

*(Dave Scoble Collection)*

The battleship *Centurion* was launched by Devonport Dockyard on 18 November 1911, and completed in 1913. Of 23,000 tons, she was armed with five twin 13.5-inch and sixteen 4-inch guns, and had a speed of 21 knots. She is seen here alongside the coaling jetty at Devonport. She took part in the Battle of Jutland in 1916. Between the wars she was disarmed and used as a radio-controlled target ship. During the Second World War she was converted to a dummy King George V Class battleship and served in the East Indies and Mediterranean. In 1944 she was again converted, this time to be a blockship, and she was deliberately sunk on 9 June 1944 as part of the harbours created off the Normandy beaches.

(*S.V. Goodman Collection*)

Two Flower class sloops are seen here moored in the River Tamar. Passing them are two 32-foot cutters under oars, doubtless from the **Impregnable** training hulks. These sloops were produced in the Great War in large numbers to a design based on the Seagull class torpedo gunboats, but incorporating much mercantile practice to permit their construction by many shipyards not normally used by the Navy. They had an average building time of 25 weeks. Designed for minesweeping, they also served as escort vessels. They had a triple hull at the bow to withstand mine or collision damage. Although they had a wide turning circle, and were lively in a seaway, they were safe and did good service. They were of 1,200 tons and were armed with two 4-inch or 12-pounder guns. Some of the class had just one funnel. Normally fitted with two masts, the mainmast could be removed to permit the ships to work kite balloons.

*(S.V. Goodman Collection)*

The battleship **Warspite**, of the Queen Elizabeth class, was launched at Devonport on 26 November 1913 and completed in April 1915. With four twin 15-inch guns, these ships had oil fired boilers. Badly damaged during the Battle of Jutland in 1916, she was soon repaired, a tribute to the Dockyard's construction. She was refitted (with a single, large funnel) in 1924-26, and underwent a major modernisation between 1934-37. She was again badly damaged in the Second World War, whilst assisting in the evacuation of Crete in 1941 and during the Salerno landings in 1943. During the Second World War she gained 14 more battle honours, the most of any RN ship. She ran aground on her way to the breakers on 23 April 1947, and was broken up in 1950.

*(S.V. Goodman Collection)*

This scene shows Atlantic Fleet destroyers lying in Devonport to give Christmas leave - probably in 1919. F55 nearest the camera was the Admiralty W class **Walker**, completed by Denny in February 1918. She was converted to a long range escort in World War II and sank **U-99** and **U-100** in March 1941. D24 was **Walrus** of the same class, completed by Fairfield in March 1918. She was to be given a full AA conversion in 1938 but was wrecked near Scarborough while on tow to be refitted. Not the sweep gear and paravanes on **Walrus**' stern.

(*T. Ferrers-Walker Collection*)

The **Courageous** had been launched as a fast cruiser (battle-cruiser) on 5 February 1916. Of 18,600 tons, she was armed with four 15-inch guns and eighteen 4-inch guns and had a speed of 31.5 knots. She was converted into an aircraft carrier at Devonport Dockyard starting in 1924. On completion she could carry 48 aircraft and carried sixteen 4.7-inch guns. She commissioned on 5 May 1928. She was sunk on 17 September 1939, having sailed from Devonport the day before, by the submarine **U-29** with the loss of 519 men. She was the first major loss of the Devonport Division during the Second World War.

*(Author's Collection)*

This general view across the River Tamar from the Naval Base in the 1920s shows the destroyers *Stormcloud* (H05), *Seabear* (H23), *Sardonyx* (H26), *Sterling* (H31) and *Tactician* (H99) lying on the Cornish side of the River by Yonderberry Oil Fuel Depot. These 'S' class destroyers were built in 1918-1919. Of 905 tons, they were armed with three 4-inch guns and had four torpedo tubes (*Tactician* has an extra two tubes fitted). Most of the class were broken up in the early 1930s, being outclassed by the larger 'V and W' destroyers, one of which lies beside Tactician. *Sardonyx*, however, was used for radar trials in 1939, and was not broken up until June 1945. An 'R' class battleship's bows can be side in midstream, with this view being taken across the quarterdeck of another battleship.

*(Dave Scoble Collection)*

On 9 August 1926 the submarine *H-29* was undergoing tests in No.2 Basin when she suddenly heeled over and, with her hatches open, sank. One Chief Engine Room Artificer and 5 dockyard workmen were lost. The water level in the basin was lowered as far as possible, but the presence of other ships prevented its being completely drained. The submarine was righted and finally raised, but the damage was so extensive that she was sold for scrap in October 1927 and broken up at Pembroke Dock. These 410-ton submarines had 4 torpedo tubes and had a speed of 13 knots surfaced and 10.5 knots dived. The first ten submarines of this class had been built in Canada, the second ten in the USA with the remainder built in Britain. Most were sold before World War II but several survived to the end of the War.

*(Author's Collection)*

The monitor *Erebus* was launched by Harland and Wolff at Govan on 19 June 1916. Of 7,200 tons, she was armed with two 15-inch guns for shore bombardment. The guns were spares for the battle-cruiser *Furious* in case her 18-inch guns failed to work. In World War I she was damaged by a distance control boat but her bulges took the impact and she was back in action in 2 weeks. She was a turret drill ship and training ship at Devonport from 1926 to 1933, with an extra deckhouse fitted forward of her turret. For four years she wore the Commander-in-Chief's Flag. In 1940 she re-commissioned and took part in several operations including Sicily, Normandy and Walcheren. She was broken up in January 1947. (*Dave Scoble Collection*)

The Barracks at Devonport, then **HMS Vivid**, was the lead establishment for introducing the general messing system into Royal Naval shore establishments. It provided the men with four good meals a day. The senior cookery specialist in *Vivid* at the time was Alfonso Jago. He was born in 1875 and joined the Navy at 16. He was the China Fleet Club lightweight boxing champion 1900-1903, and the Australian Fleet lightweight champion 1904. He was commissioned as a warrant instructor in cookery in 1911. He wrote the naval handbook of cookery in 1924-5, which was still in use in 1974. He was invalided from the Service in 1928 as a Lieutenant Instructor in Cookery. The Barracks became known as 'Jago's Mansions' as a result of his work.　　　　(*Author's Collection*)

This bleak scene shows the Barrack's canteen and theatre between the wars. Doubtless it was more convivial with large numbers of sailors present, and it provided a relief from the large dormitories in which the sailors lived and slept in the Barracks. It was also a vast improvement on the conditions that existed in the 19th Century wooden walls that formed the Barracks prior to the building of *Vivid*. The first sailors moved into the barracks from the ***Royal Adelaide*** on 4 June 1889. It was the first of all the naval shore barracks. *(Author's Collection)*

A far cry from the austerity of the barracks theatre and canteen, the wardroom of the Barracks is seen here rigged for the traditional Armada night mess dinner. The ships comprising the opposing fleets are strung from the ceiling, and the tables are laid with cutlery, glasses and silverware. Around the walls are, unusually, not paintings, but wooden carvings depicting naval events over the centuries. These were completed in May 1932 by Colonel Harold Wylie.

*(Author's Collection)*

The 'R' class battleship *Ramillies* is seen here in a floating dock in Devonport Dockyard, with the Weston Mill Lake railway bridge in the background. Of 29,150 tons, she was armed with four twin 15-inch and fourteen 6-inch guns. She was damaged during her launching by Beardmore on 12 September 1916. Capable of 22 knots, these battleships, though built after the Queen Elizabeths, were never as fast nor were they refitted to the same level, although they received some modern AA guns. *Ramillies* was damaged by a Japanese midget submarine at Madagascar, and served with the Eastern Fleet, and was at Normandy and the South of France landings. She was broken up at Cairnryan and Troon in 1948-49. One of her guns is outside the Imperial War Museum.

*(Andy Endacott Collection)*

The cruiser **Devonshire** of 9,850 tons was launched at Devonport on 22 October 1927. She completed in March 1929. The yard had previously built a half sister, **Cornwall**. **Devonshire** was armed with four twin 8-inch turrets. She was presented with a silver replica of Drake's drum on commissioning, but after several incidents, it was considered to be bad luck and was landed. She served in the Mediterranean and on the China Station before the war. In June 1940 she evacuated the King of Norway to Britain. On 22 November 1940 she sank the German raider **Atlantis**. In 1945 she was one of escorts to the King of Norway on his return to Oslo. After the war she was partly de-armed and used as the Cadets' Training Ship. She was sold for breaking up in June 1954.

*(Author's Collection)*

*Effingham* was an improved Birmingham class cruiser launched at Portsmouth on 8 June 1921, the first public launch at Portsmouth since the *Queen Elizabeth* in 1914. She completed in July 1925 with 7.5-inch guns. These ships were designed to counter German light cruisers and to run on either coal or oil, but *Effingham* was completed with 10 oil-fired boilers only. From September 1936 to September 1939 she was modernised at Devonport with nine single 6-inch guns, three tiered forward and three aft, withone each side amidships and another on the quarterdeck. On 18 May 1940 she was wrecked when she ran ashore on the Norwegian coast near Bodo. Her wreck was torpedoed where it lay to prevent salvage by the Germans.

(*T. Ferrers-Walker Collection*)

The light cruiser **Leander** was launched at Devonport on 24 September 1931, and completed in March 1933. This class of ship were fitted with four twin 6-inch guns of a new type, and had a large single funnel. She was the trial ship for welding techniques in construction. She served with the New Zealand Division of the Royal Navy from 1934-1944. During the war she sank the Italian raider **Ramb I** in February 1941, and the supply ship **Coburg** the next month. She was at Guadalcanal in September 1942 and in July 1943 was torpedoed in the forward boiler room at Kula Gulf. She had a 600 square feet hole in her side. Repairs in the USA took to 1945, by when she had returned to the Royal Navy. She was placed in reserve in 1948 and broken up at Blyth in 1950.

*(Author's Collection)*

The light cruiser *Apollo* was launched at Devonport on 9 October 1934. Like *Leander* she was armed with four twin 6-inch guns, but she had a different machinery layout resulting in two separate funnels. She completed in January 1936 and carried out one commission in the Royal Navy before transferring to the Royal Australian Navy as the *Hobart* on 13 October 1938. In July 1943 she was torpedoed by the Japanese submarine *I-11* off the New Hebrides. She was repaired in time to be at the Japanese surrender in Tokyo Bay. Post war a major modernisation was started, but abandoned. She was sold to be broken up in Japan in February 1962.

*(Author's Collection)*

The Southampton class cruiser **Birmingham** was launched at Devonport on 1 September 1936, and completed in November 1937.  These handsome ships carried four triple 6-inch and four twin 4-inch guns.  **Birmingham** was unusual for RN cruisers in having no knuckle in her bow.  She took part in the Norwegian campaign in 1940 and operations in the Indian Ocean and Mediterranean.  In November 1943 she was badly damaged by a submarine torpedo off Cyrenaica, repairs taking place at Newport, Virginia and Portsmouth to 1945.  In 1950-52 she was modernised with a lattice mast forward and modern AA fire control directors, as seen here.  She was broken up at Inverkeithing in September 1960.        *(T. Ferrers-Walker Collection)*

The minesweeper **Sharpshooter** was launched at Devonport on 10 December 1936 and completed in December 1937. She was of the Halcyon class, 835 tons, armed with two 4-inch guns and capable of 17 knots. Six ships of this class were built at Devonport. She was damaged in a collision during the Dunkirk evacuation and had to be towed to Dover. She served on Russian convoys sinking **U-685** by ramming on 24 March 1942 while escorting convoy QP 9 from Russia. In 1946 she was converted to a survey ship and operated in the Far East. In 1948-52 she worked off Lowestoft and in 1953 was renamed **Shackleton** and continued survey duties in home waters. She returned to Devonport for the last time on 9 November 1962 and was broken up at Troon in November 1965.                         (*S.V. Goodman Collection*)

The destroyer *Javelin* was one of the most modern destroyers to be completed before the outbreak of World War II. Launched on 21 December 1938 on the Clyde, she completed in June 1939. Of 1,690 tons, she was armed with three twin 4.7-inch guns and ten torpedo tubes. On the night 28/29 November 1940 she and her sister ship *Jackal* were in action with three German destroyers 20 miles off the Lizard. *Javelin* was torpedoed by the German destroyer *Hans Lody*. One torpedo struck just forward of 'A' gun and blew off her bow, another struck by the after superstructure and took off her stern, as can be seen in the photo. 48 of her crew were lost

(*T. Ferrers-Walker Collection*)

After her damage *Javelin* was towed into Devonport. Only 155ft of her original 353 ft of hull remained. Repairs took until December 1941, and she was pictured here shortly afterwards, looking as good as new - a tribute to the skills of the Dockyard workforce. She had already gained 3 battle honours in the war, and went on to gain a further 5 ranging from Diego Suarez to the Arctic during the war. Of the 8 ships of the 'J' class, only *Jervis* and *Javelin* survived the war – typical of the loss rate of the hard worked destroyers in the early war years.

*(Dave Scoble Collection)*

The French battleship *Paris* is seen here in the Prince of Wales Basin, with the drill shed of the Barracks in the background. Launched in September 1912, she was of 22,189 tons displacement and was armed with twelve 12–inch guns. She was, when the war started, about to be replaced by modern battleships then building in France. She, together with other French warships, was seized on 3 July 1940 at Plymouth lest they fell into German hands. She was commissioned 9 days later to be a depot ship for Polish personnel on the Tyne. However, this was cancelled and she became a depot ship for Auxiliary Patrol personnel at Devonport in the place of the old battleship *Centurion*. She paid off on 30 June 1945 and was returned to the French Navy on 14 July 1945.

*(S.V. Goodman Collection)*

The cruiser **Exeter** was launched at Devonport on 18 July 1929, and completed in February 1931. She was the last British heavy cruiser built, and was armed with three twin 8-inch guns. There were just two ships of this class built, **Exeter** differing from her sister ship (**York**) in having upright funnels and masts, and a new style bridge structure. During the pre-war years she operated on the America and West Indies Station. In December 1939 she was one of three cruisers that cornered the German pocket battleship **Graf Spee** off the River Plate. During the action she suffered severe damage and heavy casualties. She is seen here on her return to Devonport on 15 February 1940. The barge in the right foreground carried Winston Churchill who greeted the ship's company on their triumphant return.

*(Dave Scoble Collection)*

The *Exeter* is seen here in Plymouth Sound after repairs to her action damage. Opportunity had been taken to improve her AA defences by fitting twin 4-inch guns and multiple pom-poms, and to fit tripod masts to support radar aerials. She re-commissioned on 10 March 1941, and left Devonport 14 days later - before her refit was fully completed- in order to avoid the heavy air raids taking place on Plymouth at that time. She sailed for service in the Far East and in February 1942 was damaged in the Battle of Java Sea. On 1 March 1942, whilst trying to retire from the Java Sea, she encountered a large force of Japanese heavy cruisers and destroyers and was sunk. The survivors then suffered over three years in captivity from which not all returned.

*(Author's Collection)*

The destroyer **USS Sigournay** of 1917 was handed over to the Royal Navy at Halifax on 26 November 1940. She was renamed **Newport** nine days later. She sailed for Devonport via Belfast, where she was damaged in an air raid. She refitted at Devonport from January to September 1941, and then commissioned with a Norwegian crew. She is seen here in Plymouth Sound just after re-commissioning. In March 1942 she collided with her sister ship **Beverley**, and repairs took fourteen months. She re-commissioned into the Royal Navy, but was no longer required as an escort so became an air target ship. She paid off in July 1945 and arrived at Granton on 18 February 1947 to be broken up.    (*Dave Scoble Collection*)

This general view of the North Yard during World War II can be dated as April 1941 because it shows the old battleship **Centurion** in dry dock. She had been built at Devonport, and between the wars was used as a target ship. From 1940-41 she became a base ship for trawlers in the Devonport area. That task was transferred to the French battleship **Paris** in April 1941. Then, in just two weeks, despite heavy air raids taking place, she was converted in a dummy King George V class battleship. In the foreground is an 'S' class destroyer, either **Sardonyx** or **Sturdy**. Across the jetty from her lies a modern ('J' class?) destroyer, with, on the opposite side of that basin, the 'R' class tug **Retort**. **Retort** operated from Devonport from completion in 1918 until 1952, and was sold in September 1958.

(*S.V. Goodman Collection*)

The light cruiser *Gloucester* is seen here running trials without her gunnery director or AA guns.  She was launched at Devonport on 19 October 1937, and completed in January 1939.  Of 9,400 tons, she was a half sister to the ***Birmingham***, being armed with four triple 6-inch guns.  After trials and work up she joined the East Indies Station.  In 1940 she was transferred to the Mediterranean.  In July 1940 her Captain and 17 others were killed when she was bombed south of Crete.  In January 1941 she was hit by a bomb, which fortunately failed to explode.  Her sister ship, ***Southampton***, in company with her, was not so fortunate and caught fire and had to be sunk by her.  She took part in the Battle of Matapan, and on 22 May, 1941, during the operations to defend Crete, she and the cruiser *Fiji* were caught in heavy and sustained air attacks and both ships were sunk.  Over 700 of her crew were lost, yet another severe blow to the Devonport Port Division.

*(Author's Collection)*

The 26,500-ton battle-cruiser **Repulse** was launched in January 1916 and completed seven months later. In November 1917 she was in action in the Heligoland Bight and hit the German **Konigsberg** with her 15-inch gunfire. In 1917 she became the first capital ship to carry an aircraft on her turret. Although armour plate had been added after the Great War, and from 1933-36 she underwent a major refit, by 1939 her anti-aircraft defences were inadequate for modern warfare. She covered convoys across the Atlantic; took part in the Norwegian campaign and joined the hunt for the **Bismarck**. In 1941, with no break from relentless war operations, she was sent to boost the defences in the Far East. On 10 December 1941 she, and the battleship **Prince of Wales**, were attacked by large numbers of Japanese aircraft. Both ships were sunk. **Repulse** lost 436 officers and men, and **Prince of Wales** 328. Both ships were manned by the Devonport Port Division.

*(Author's Collection)*

This is a view of 2 and 3 Basins in 1941. In the foreground lies the destroyer **Stanley** (ex **USS McCalla)**. This 1919 destroyer had been commissioned into the Royal Navy on 23 October 1940, and then underwent a major refit at Devonport. The forward boilers were removed together with two funnels to provide extra fuel stowage, and a new British destroyer bridge was fitted. On completion in September 1941 she was one of the most effective long-range escorts available. She joined the Liverpool Sloop Division and later transferred to the 40th Escort Group under Captain Walker. In December 1941, whilst escorting convoy HG76, she sank **U-131** and **U-434**, but was torpedoed by **U-574** on 19 December. There were only 24 survivors. **U-574** was sunk shortly afterwards by **Stork**.

(*S.V. Goodman Collection*)

The Colony class cruiser *Trinidad* was launched at Devonport on 21 March 1940, and completed in October 1941. She is seen here in Plymouth Sound soon after completion, with four triple 6-inch and four twin 4-inch guns. On 29 March 1942, whilst escorting a convoy to Russia, she was damaged in an action with three German destroyers. One of the German destroyers (*Z26*) was sunk, but *Trinidad* was hit by one of her own torpedoes which did not run straight. Temporary repairs were carried at Murmansk. On 13 May 1942 she sailed for the UK with an escort of four destroyers. The force came under heavy bombing attacks on the next day, and *Trinidad* was hit and badly disabled. She had to be abandoned and sunk by the destroyer *Matchless* early on 15th.

*(Author's Collection)*

This photograph purports to show the destroyer *Hotspur* in dry dock in Devonport after ramming a submarine in September 1943. Certainly it shows an escort in North Atlantic camouflage paint with a damaged bow. However, this does not tie in with **Hotspur's** movement records. **Hotspur**, completed in December 1936, was badly damaged at the first Battle of Narvik in a collision with her sister ship **Hunter**. On 20 October 1940 she rammed and sank the submarine **Lafole**, but repairs were carried out at Gibraltar and Malta. She took part in the Battle of Matapan and helped sink **U-79** on 23 December 1941. She returned to Plymouth on 27 February 1943, but then refitted at Sheerness to become an escort destroyer, with reduced gunnery armament and extra radar. In August/September 1943 she was operating between St. Johns (Canada) and Londonderry. She became the Dominican **Trujillo** in 1948, renamed **Duarte** in 1962 and was deleted in 1972. Nevertheless, it does show typical damage to the Royal Navy's ships during the war, and Devonport Dockyard was called upon to repair it. In the first 18 months of the war, Devonport carried out over 200 repairs to destroyers. *(S.V. Goodman Collection)*

The 'T' class submarine *Torbay* is seen lying off Plymouth Breakwater between commissions in the Mediterranean. She was launched at Chatham Dockyard on 9 April 1940 and completed in November 1940. She sank the Italian submarine *Jantina* in July 1941. Four of these 1,090-ton class of submarines were built by Devonport Dockyard. They carried a 4-inch and a 20-mm gun, and had ten torpedo tubes. *Torbay* served in the Mediterranean in 1941-43, and also operated in Arctic waters and off Malaya. She arrived at Briton Ferry to be broken up in January 1946.

*(Author's Collection)*

The trawler **Rowan** is seen here off net defences in Plymouth Sound, with Stadden Heights in the background. These Tree class trawlers were ordered in July 1939, when the shortage of warships for the task ahead was clear. Of 530 tons, she was armed with a 12-pounder gun forward and had two 0.5-inch AA guns and machine guns. She had a speed of 11.5 knots. **Rowan** was launched by Smith's Dock on 12 August 1939, and she survived the war to became the mercantile **Maiken** in 1947. These trawlers were used for anti-submarine and minesweeping duties and were in such short supply that hundreds were requisitioned from civilian resources.

*(Dave Scoble Collection)*

The 'T' class submarine *Tigris* is seen here off Drake's Island. She had been launched on 31 October 1939 at Chatham Dockyard and completed in June 1940. These were patrol type submarines with a 42-day endurance. They had a range of 11,000 miles at 10 knots. She sank the Italian submarines *Thorn* on 2 April 1941 and *Porfido* on 6 December 1942. However, she was lost on 10 March 1943 on a patrol which was to the South West of Naples. The first of this class (*Triton*) was completed in 1938. Many of the class were operational after the war and were modernised and survived into the 1970s.

(*Dave Scoble Collection*)

General Wladyslav Sikorsky was born on 2 May 1881, and was Prime Minister of Poland when it was over-run by the Germans in 1939. He escaped to London and became the Head of the Polish Government in exile. He was killed in an air crash off Gibraltar on 4 July 1943. His body was brought back to Devonport on 10 July in the Polish destroyer *Orkan* (ex *HMS Myrmidon*), and his coffin is seen here being brought ashore at Devonport with a Polish guard of honour. Sadly, the *Orkan* was sunk by a U-boat on 8 October that year with just 44 survivors.

*(S.V. Goodman Collection)*

The Hunt class destroyer *Cleveland* is seen lying in Plymouth Sound. She was launched on 24 April 1940 by Yarrow and completed in September 1940. Of 907 tons, these small destroyers were armed with a twin 4-inch gun forward, and one aft. They also carried a quadruple 3-pounder in X position, aft of the searchlight. They were designed for three twin 4-inch and torpedo tubes, but initial trials showed these were too heavy for their light hulls. They had a designed speed of 30 knots, though at sea their maximum was nearer 26 knots. 86 of these small destroyers (later classed as frigates) were built. They were a valuable supplement to the Royal Navy's strength during the war. *Cleveland* was involved in several convoy actions off the coast near Plymouth, shooting down one aircraft and driving off E-boats. She survived the war and was sold for breaking up in 1957. She was wrecked on Rhossili Sands on her way to the breakers and the wreck was destroyed in 1959.

(*Dave Scoble Collection*)

The cruiser ***Orion*** was launched by Devonport Dockyard on 24 November 1932, and was completed on 18 January 1934. A sister ship to the ***Leander*** (*page 36*), pre-war she served in the Home Fleet and in the West Indies. In May 1940 she joined the Mediterranean Fleet and took part in many actions. She was badly damaged during the evacuation from Crete. She is seen here in Plymouth Sound after repairs, with tripod masts and twin 4-inch guns. She returned to the Mediterranean for the landings in Sicily, Salerno and Anzio. At Normandy she fired 3,358 shells between 6 and 12 June 1944. She then returned to the Mediterranean for the landings in the South of France and to cover the return to Greece. She gained a massive 13 Battle Honours in the war. In 1949 she was used for trials in Loch Striven, and was broken up at Troon later that year.

(*Dave Scoble Collection*)

The battlecruiser **Renown** was launched on 4 March 1916 by Fairfield and completed in September 1916. She was modernised just prior to WWII with new machinery. The weight saved allowed her to be given more armour and an effective AA defence of twenty 4.5-inch guns. She served in the Norwegian campaign and with Force H in 1940-41, taking part in the search for the **Bismarck**. In 1944-45 she was with the Eastern Fleet, but was recalled to the Home Fleet, covering 7,600 miles in less than 15 days, lest the German major warships tried a last break out. In May 1945 her complement was reduced and on 2 August 1945 was in Plymouth Sound with the US cruisers **Augusta** and **Philadelphia** for the meeting of King George VI with President Harry Truman, who landed at Yelverton Airfield. This scene shows **Renown** flying the various standards for this meeting. **Renown** then joined the **Imperieuse** training group in the Hamoaze. In December 1946 she was placed in reserve at Devonport and on 8 August 1948 she arrived at Faslane to be broken up. (*Andy Endacott Collection*)

The **Terrible** was the only aircraft carrier built in a Royal Dockyard. She was laid down in April 1943 and launched on 30 September 1944. Of 15,700 tons, she was a light fleet carrier armed with twenty-eight 40-mm guns and could carry 35 aircraft. She had a speed of 24.5knots. Work on her slowed once the war ended, but she was completed in February 1949. In December 1948 she had been transferred to the Royal Australian Navy and been renamed **Sydney**. She took part in the Korean War, attended the Coronation Review at Spithead and became a training ship in 1955. In 1961 she was modified to be a fast transport and she finally paid off in November 1973. She left Sydney on 23 December 1975 to be broken up in South Korea. A second carrier, **Polythemus**, had been ordered from Devonport in 1942, but was never laid down, being cancelled in 1945.                                              (*Dave Scoble Collection*)

After the war the Navy found itself with too many ships and too few men. A large number of ships were laid up in rivers and creeks around the United Kingdom. In this view the ***Albrighton*** is seen alongside a fleet destroyer and a frigate in the River Tamar. ***Albrighton*** was in the third group of Hunt class destroyers (later rated as frigates) and had been at Dieppe and Normandy. In 1959 she was transferred to the Germany Navy as the ***Raule*** and was not broken up until 1969. Many other ships in reserve went directly to the breakers, but some were refitted and served in the Royal Navy again. In the 1950s the ships that were being retained were put into a proper state of preservation.

(*Author's Collection*)

Though not of the best quality, this general view of the River Tamar north of the Royal Albert Bridge in the late 1940s/early 1950s, shows the size of the Reserve Fleet. Included in the ships are fleet and Hunt class destroyers and frigates. In 1950 the Reserve Fleet organisations were given names, *Orion* being chosen for Devonport, ***Bellerophon*** for Portsmouth, ***Mars*** for Harwich, *Neptune* for Chatham, and ***Cochrane*** for Rosyth. A series of Headquarters ships were allocated, and in 1966 the ***Tyne*** took on the role in Devonport, and the name ***Orion*** dropped. These headquarters were also responsible for the many ships laid up in commercial ports.

(*T. Ferrers-Walker Collection*)

The destroyer *Porcupine* was completed on the Tyne in August 1942. She was armed with five 4-inch guns of an old style due to shortages of modern 4.7-inch guns. She also carried four torpedo tubes. On 9 December 1942 she was torpedoed by *U-602* in the Mediterranean, and was towed in two halves to harbour. Each part was used as a depot ship, being given the names *Pork* and *Pine* respectively by their ship's companies. The bow section was taken to Plymouth for breaking up in May 1946, and the stern section was demolished at Southampton.

(*T. Ferrers-Walker Collection*)

The *Ace* was an 'A' class submarine laid down on 3 December 1943 at Devonport and launched on 14 March 1945. With the ending of the war, she was never completed, but was used for trials in Loch Striven from 1948-50, and then broken up at Port Glasgow in June 1950. A second of this class, designed for Pacific Ocean operations, the *Achates*, was launched at Devonport on 20 September 1945. She too was never completed, but was used for trials of hull strength off Gibraltar. Her hull collapsed during these trials and she was sunk two miles south of Europa Point as an Asdic target. *(Dave Scoble Collection)*

The monitor **Roberts**, of 7,970 tons, was armed with two 15-inch guns, originally fitted to the **Marshal Soult**. She also carried eight 4-inch and lighter AA guns. She was launched on 1 February 1941 on the Clyde and completed in July 1941. She took part in the North African, Sicilian and Salerno landings, being damaged by bombing in November 1942 and July 1943. She then took part in the Normandy and Walcheren operations. She returned from the Far East in November 1945 and became a turret drill ship at Devonport and later was used as an accommodation and fender ship, alongside the North Wall. In 1963 she was taken out and laid up in the River Tamar and finally left Devonport on 19 July 1965 to be broken up at Inverkeithing.

*(Dave Scoble Collection)*

In November 1943 the old battleships *Revenge* and *Resolution* were commissioned as *Shrapnel II* at Southampton to train stokers. In April 1944 they were steamed to Gareloch to clear the area for the Normandy landings. In Scotland they were called *Imperieuse II*. In December 1944 they moved to Devonport to continue their training task. Later they were joined by the battlecruiser *Renown*, carrier *Unicorn* and battleship *Valiant*, all under the collective name of *Imperieuse*. This view shows the array of capital ships forming *Imperieuse* at the north end of the Hamoaze prior to paying off in late 1947.

(*T. Ferrers-Walker Collection*)

The King George V class battleship *Anson* is seen approaching Devil's Point on her way up harbour to Devonport Dockyard. She was launched on 24 February 1940 by Swan Hunter, and completed in June 1942. She covered Russian convoy operations and strikes against targets in Norway. In 1944 she went to the Far East, and was present at the surrender of the Japanese in Hong Kong in September 1945. Armed with ten 14-inch guns and sixteen 5.25-inch guns, *Anson* was the only one of the class to be refitted with modern AA gunnery directors, visible just forward of her foremast. Returning to the UK in 1946, she joined the Training Squadron, operating in the Channel. She was laid up in 1950 in the Gareloch and was broken up at Faslane in December 1957.

(*Steve Bush Collection*)

The fleet aircraft carrier **Victorious** was launched in September 1939 and completed in April 1941. She immediately took part in the search for the **Bismarck**. After covering convoys to Malta and the North African landings she served in the Pacific and then returned to the UK for operations against targets in Norway. In 1945 she served in the Pacific again, being hit by Kamikaze aircraft. She was used for trooping duties after the war, then joined the Training Squadron at Portland. She is seen here leaving Devonport for Portsmouth prior to a major refit, which lasted from 1950-58. Then, completely modernised, she served until 1967, paying off for a refit. In 1967 she suffered a fire during her refit which led to her premature decommissioning. She arrived at Faslane on 15 July 1969 to be broken up. *(S.V. Goodman Collection)*

This general view of the Prince of Wales Basin in the 1950s shows work progressing on the facilities alongside the docks. In the basin are two aircraft carriers, and also a large number of smaller ships comprising a small part of the Reserve Fleet. Included are the netlayer **Protector**, a Battle class fleet destroyer, a 'T' class Type 16 frigate, a maintenance ship and an Algerine class ocean minesweeper. In the far distance are the huts and masts of the old boys training establishment **Impregnable** at Bull Point, which paid off in 1948 and was then used to accommodate WRNS. A third carrier can be seen at 8 wharf by the coaling jetty.

(*Dave Scoble Collection*)

The **Alaunia**, a Cunard Steam Ship Co. liner launched in 1925, had been requisitioned as an armed merchant cruiser in August 1939. She was converted to be a repair ship from 1942-45 and commissioned for duty in the Far East in August 1945. She was placed in reserve in 1946, but in June 1947 became a training ship for engine room ratings at Devonport. She is seen here lying in midstream just off Bull Point with the old **Impregnable** establishment in the background. She paid off in October 1956 and in September 1957 was towed to Blyth to be broken up.

*(Author's Collection)*

The corvette **Carisbrooke Castle** was launched on 31 July 1943 by Caledon and completed in November 1943. These ships were a major improvement on the Flower class corvettes, having the very effective Squid anti-submarine mortar forward of the bridge. These 1,060 tons ships were built by shipyards too small to build the larger, faster frigates. She was placed in reserve at Devonport from 1947-52, and then commissioned for the Second Frigate Squadron operating from Portland. She attended the Spithead Review in 1953. She is seen here passing the Torpoint Ferry with a County class cruiser in the background. She paid off to reserve at Devonport in November 1956 when relieved by a modern Type 14 frigate. She arrived at Faslane on 11 June 1958 to be broken up.

(*Author's Collection*)

The 'S' class submarine **Sentinel** is seen conducting trials in the Prince of Wales Basin. Launched on 27 July 1945 and completed in December 1945, she was the last of her class to be launched. Of 715 tons and with a speed of 14.75 knots on the surface and 9 knots when dived, she is seen here fitted with snort which allowed her to use her diesel engines whilst submerged. Beyond her lies the fleet destroyer **Cambrian**, completed in July 1944 by Scotts. She was armed with four 4.5-inch guns, but was later modernised with an enclosed bridge and squid anti-submarine mortars in place of her X gun. Beyond can be seen the Barracks with the clock tower and drill shed. (*S.V. Goodman Collection*)

The 'A' class submarine **Alliance** is seen here in No. 7 Dock (off 1 Basin in North Yard) during a refit in 1960. She was launched on 28 July 1945 at Barrow, and completed in May 1947. Of 1,120 tons, these submarines were of all welded construction and had a range of 11,500 miles at 11 knots. In the 1950s they were given streamlined hulls and fins (conning towers) to make them faster and quieter, and **Alliance** is seen here in her new guise. In February 1978 she was handed over to the Submarine Museum at Gosport. She was put ashore in June 1981 and is now a permanent exhibit at the Museum. No. 7 Dock was part of the area taken into use for the covered docks, which opened in 1977.

(*S.V. Goodman Collection*)

The aircraft carrier *Unicorn* is seen her on 17 November 1953 returning from operations during the Korean War. Beyond her lie ships of the Reserve Fleet, and to the left is the bow of the carrier *Indefatigable*. *Unicorn* had been launched at Belfast on 20 November 1940, and completed in 1943. Designed as an aircraft supply and repair ship, she was used operationally at Salerno, and in the Eastern Fleet became a deck landing training ship. She was with the Fleet Train in the British Pacific Fleet in 1945. In 1946 she was placed in reserve at Devonport and was part of the *Imperieuse* training establishment to March 1948. During the Korean War she carried thousands of passengers of all 3 Services. In 1954 she was placed in extended Reserve at Devonport before being broken up at Dalmuir and Troon 1959-60. The tugs in attendance are the *Pert*, *Camel* and *Exhorter*. (*Dave Scoble Collection*)

The battleship *Vanguard* is seen here arriving at Devonport in 1946. She refitted at Devonport in 1946-47 and again in 1954-55. Launched on 30 November 1944 by John Brown, she completed in April 1946. Of 44,500 tons, to speed construction during the war years she was armed with four old twin 15-inch guns first mounted in the battle-cruisers *Courageous* and *Glorious*. She also had eight twin 5.25-inch and many smaller AA guns. She took part in the Royal Tour to South Africa and in 1949 became Flagship of the Training Squadron. After her second refit at Devonport she was placed in reserve. She was towed to Faslane from Portsmouth on 9 August 1960 to be broken up. (*Andy Endacott Collection*)

The battleship ***Howe*** is seen here entering the Prince of Wales Basin. ***Howe*** was launched on 9 April 1940 by Fairfield, and completed in June 1942. She covered Russian convoys and the landings in Sicily. She was at Taranto for the surrender there. In 1944 she was with the Eastern Fleet and in 1945 with the British Pacific Fleet, bombarding the Japanese positions in May 1945 at Okinawa. She returned to the UK in January 1946 and joined the Training Squadron. She was Senior Officer of the Reserve Fleet at Devonport from May 1949-October 1952 and was then placed in reserve in the Hamoaze. She was towed from Devonport on 27 May 1958 for breaking up at Inverkeithing. Visible over the forward massive quadruple 14-inch gun turret of ***Howe*** is her sister ship ***King George V***, with destroyers, the training group of ships ***Defiance*** at Wilcove, and aircraft carriers in reserve. (*S. V. Goodman Collection*)

The ***Tremadoc Bay*** was photographed in the summer of 1947 coming alongside her sister ship ***Burghead Bay***, with Mount Edgcumbe in the background. Both ships were returning from duty escorting refugee ships during the Palestine operations. These 1,580-ton frigates were the anti-aircraft variant of the Loch class. They carried two twin 4-inch guns and six 40-mm guns. Prefabricated for rapid construction, ***Tremadoc Bay*** was launched on 29 March 1945 and completed that October by Harland and Wolff, ***Burghead Bay*** was launched on 3 March 1945 by Hill of Bristol and completed in September 1945. ***Tremadoc Bay*** was part of the Devonport Local Flotilla from 1945-51 and was then put into Reserve at Devonport, and later Gibraltar, before being broken up at Genoa in September 1953. ***Burghead Bay*** was in the local Flotilla from completion to 1952. She then served on the South Atlantic Station before going into reserve at Devonport in 1958. She was sold to Portugal in May 1959 and renamed ***Alvares Cabral***. She was sold in June 1971. *(S.V. Goodman Collection)*

The *Snipe* is seen here returning to Devonport from the West Indies on 26 October 1950 with her paying off pendant flying and families on the jetty ready to greet her ship's company. A modified Black Swan class sloop (later classed a frigate) of 1,350 tons, she was armed with three twin 4-inch and six 40-mm guns. She was launched by Denny on 20 December 1945 and completed in September 1946. These excellent AA ships were equipped with Denny Brown roll reducers (stabilizers) and had a good endurance of 7,500 miles at 12 knots. *Snipe* served in the West Indies from 1946-1952. In 1953 she operated off the Falkland Islands, returning to Devonport on 28 May 1953 to pay off to reserve. She was towed from reserve at Barry on 23 August 1960 to be broken up at Newport.

*(S.V. Goodman Collection)*

The *Veryan Bay* is seen her returning to Devonport to pay off. Her Hedgehog anti-submarine mortar can be seen just aft of the cable party on the forecastle, and her forward twin 4-inch gun has racks for firing flares on each side. She was launched on 11 November 1944 by Hill of Bristol, and completed in May 1945. She went direct to the Far East, returning in 1947 to join the Second Frigate Squadron in the Mediterranean. From 1949 to 1957 she carried out several commissions on the America and West Indies Station with refits at Devonport between. She then was placed in reserve at Devonport and was towed away on 19 June 1959 to be broken up at Charlestown.

*(S.V. Goodman Collection)*

The *Amethyst* achieved fame when she was fired upon by Chinese guns on the Yangtse on 20 April 1949. Twenty two of her crew were killed and thirty one others injured. She was forced to anchor, but on 30 July she set out down river and was met the next day by the destroyer *Concord*. She is seen here arriving at Devonport to a tumultuous welcome. She was a Modified Black Swan class sloop (later rated frigate) of 1,350 tons, launched on 7 May 1943 by Stephen and completed in October 1943. She assisted in the sinking of two submarines before being transferred to the Far East in 1945. She served in the Far East until 1953, including service in the Korean War. She was placed in reserve in 1954, and in 1956 was used in the making of the film '*The Yangtse Incident*'. She arrived at Plymouth in January 1947 to be broken up. *(Andy Endacaott Collection)*

The heavy cruiser **Devonshire** is seen here in December 1954 passing the slip on which she had been launched in October 1927 on her last voyage to the breaker's yard at Newport. She had retained just the forward twin 8-inch gun whilst acting as Cadets' Training Ship from April 1947 to August 1953. She was relieved in that role by the light fleet carrier **Triumph**. She was being moved by the Samson class tug **Superman** (alongside), completed in 1954, and the Nimble class tug **Careful** (astern), completed in 1946. (*Dave Scoble Collection*)

This was a forlorn sight, the north west corner of the Prince of Wales basin with a motley collection of motor boats and motor fishing vessels in secure shelter from the south west gales. The coaling wharf still retained coal. But it was soon all to change. The coal was cleared and the associated cranes and other equipment removed, and a new Fleet Maintenance Base built. It completed in 1978 after 6 years work. The Submarine Refit Complex was to be completed on the northern wall of the Basin in May 1980 after 7 years work. In 1986 work started on the Weston Mill Lake jetty beyond. This scene would be unrecognisable to a modern dockyard worker or sailor.                  (*Andy Endicott Collection*)

Albert Gate opened into the south end of the North Dockyard by No. 1 Basin. In this view it had been surmounted with a model of Sir Francis Drake's ship, the **Golden Hind**, as part of the Coronation celebrations in 1953. There is floodlighting for the model, and the Royal Cypher directly above the actual gate is fitted with lamps for illumination. The Dockyard Policeman stands sentinel by his small shelter. From 1860 to 1934 the security of the Yard was the responsibility of the Metropolitan Police. The Royal Marine Police then took over. The Admiralty Constabulary was formed in 1949, later becoming the Ministry of Defence Police. Later the Dockyard boundaries were extended to include new office blocks, and the old gate, based on a design by Mr. William Scamp, was closed on 4 September 1966 after a new wall had been completed around the new perimeter. *(Andy Endacott Collection)*

The frigate *Venus* started life as a fleet destroyer of 1,710 tons. She was launched by Fairfield on 23 February 1943, and took part in actions in the Arctic, at Normandy and in the East Indies. After the war the Navy was short of fast anti-submarine vessels to cope with the threat posed by faster submarines, so many destroyers were modernised to turn them into anti-submarine frigates. *Venus* was typical. The major refit involved stripping her upperworks completely, and was carried out by Devonport Dockyard in 1951-52. She later acted as escort to the Cadets' training ship *Triumph* prior to becoming one of the founder members of the Dartmouth Training Squadron. She was thus a frequent visitor to Devonport. After paying off she was used as a target and finally arrived at Briton Ferry on 20 December 1972 to be broken up. (*Steve Bush Collection*)

***Motor Fishing Vessel 1204*** was used as a depot ship for midget submarines, and was named ***Escort***. On her funnel is the number 5, indicating she was part of the Fifth Submarine Flotilla. Alongside her, in this view, taken as she lay off ***Defiance*** at Wilcove, is the midget submarine ***XE8***. These small, 30.3 ton submarines could carry two side charges, each with 2 tons of explosive, and were used to good effect in the war, attacking both German and Japanese heavy ships. They also were used to mark the beaches for D-Day at Normandy and to cut telegraph cables in the Far East. ***XE8*** was sunk as a bottom target in 1954, but was raised in May 1973 and taken to Chatham Dockyard to be preserved. *(Author's Collection)*

The air direction frigate **Salisbury** is seen here in No. 2 Basin shortly after her launching at Devonport on 25 June 1953. She was completed in February 1957. Armed with a twin 4.5-inch gun forward, her main equipment comprised radar arrays and offices aft to allow her to control aircraft and assist in aircraft carrier operations. She was the first warship built by Devonport Dockyard post-war, and had diesel propulsion. She paid off on 30 June 1978. A sale to Egypt was not completed. From 1980-85 she lay in the Hamoaze as a training ship for ratings from the training establishment **Raleigh**. She ended her days being sunk as a target West of Ireland on 30 December 1985. *(Dave Scoble Collection)*

The cruiser *Nigeria* is seen her laid up at the buoys just north of the Torpoint Ferry in 1950-51. This 8,000-ton Colony class cruiser was launched on the Tyne on 18 July 1939 and completed in September 1940. She served in northern waters, the Mediterranean and East Indies. In August 1942 she was severely damaged by a submarine torpedo whilst on a Malta Convoy. Repairs were carried out in the USA to July 1943. From 1946-50 she was the Flagship on the South Atlantic Station. In December 1950 she joined the Reserve Fleet at Devonport, remaining there until August 1951, when she went to Rosyth as an accommodation ship. In 1954 she was purchased by India and underwent a refit, being renamed *Mysore* in August 1957. She finally paid off on 29 August 1985 and was deleted in 1986.

*(S.V. Goodman Collection)*

This photograph of the cruiser **Royalist** was taken in Plymouth Sound on completion of a major modernisation carried out in Devonport Dockyard between 1954 and April 1956. The 5,900-ton cruiser of the modified Dido class had been launched on 30 May 1942 by Scotts and completed in September 1943. She was used as an escort carrier squadron flagship, and served in northern waters, Mediterranean, Aegean and East Indies. During her extensive refit she was fitted with a new bridge, lattice masts, new fire control system for her four twin 5.25-inch guns and a new secondary armament. In July 1956 she transferred to the Royal New Zealand Navy, and took part in operations in Malaya in 1957-58. She paid off in 1966 and arrived at Kure, Japan, to be broken up on 13 February 1968.

*(Author's Collection)*

This aerial photograph shows the Prince of Wales Basin and associated graving docks. This non-tidal area of 35 acres was completed in 1907. At the same time No. 4 basin (nearer the camera) was built. In this photograph, believed to be taken about 1959, are four aircraft carriers, including **Eagle**, **Hermes**, and a Centaur class light fleet carrier. The cruiser **Belfast**, just completing a major refit, is on the south wall of No. 4 Basin, with two modern frigates on the East wall. Another cruiser and a destroyer are alongside in Weston Mill Lake at the top of the picture. The **Ark Royal** is undergoing her major 1959-61 refit. A fleet replenishment ship and a landing ship (tank) are in the graving docks. The depot ship **Tyne** lies just beyond the cranes of the coaling wharf in the northwest corner of the Yard.

*(Author's Collection)*

The Rothesay class frigate **Plymouth** was launched at Devonport on 20 July 1959, and completed in May 1961. Of 2,380 tons, she was 370 feet long and armed with a twin 4.5-inch gun and Limbo anti-submarine mortars. In 1960-69 she was modernised to carry a helicopter. She took a major part in the Falklands War of 1982, and finally paid off in April 1988. She is seen here entering Plymouth Sound to visit before paying off for the last time. She was retained for preservation at Plymouth and later Glasgow. In 1990 she was sold to the Warship Preservation Trust and in 1992 she was moved to Birkenhead to be open to visitors.

*(MoD/Crown Copyright)*

Shortly after ***Plymouth*** was launched, the next frigate was laid down at Devonport. ***Tartar*** was a Tribal class general-purpose frigate, to be armed with two single 4.5-inch guns, a Limbo anti-submarine mortar and a helicopter. She was launched on 19 July 1960, and makes a brave sight in this photograph as she goes down the slipway. These ships were flush deck and introduced dining halls for ratings in small ships. They also had a combined steam and gas turbine system of propulsion for their single propeller. Completed in 1963, she served mainly in the North Atlantic and Home waters, carrying out fishery protection duties in 1975. She was put in the Stand-by Squadron (Reserve) at Chatham in 1980. She was sold in April 1984 to Indonesia, renamed ***Hasanuddin*** in 1985 and deleted in 2000.

(*S.V. Goodman Collection*)

The next ship to be laid down at Devonport was the Leander class frigate **Cleopatra**, on 19 June 1963. She was launched on 25 March 1964 and completed in March 1966. Of 2,650 tons, these ships were a development of the Rothesay class frigates, but were flush decked and fitted to operate helicopters, with a hangar and flight deck aft. **Cleopatra** served in the Far East and also took part in the Cod War of 1973. In 1974 she was modified at Devonport with the Exocet missile system, the first of her class to be so fitted. She is photographed here in that guise. She later served in the West Indies and Far East. In 1982-83 she was again modernised, being fitted with a towed array anti-submarine system. She paid off in January 1992 and arrived at Alang to be broken up in January 1994.

*(Author's Collection)*

The *Scylla*, a sister ship to *Cleopatra*, was laid down on 17 May 1967 and launched on 8 August 1968, the last warship to be built in Devonport Dockyard. The Yard had also built another sister ship, *Danae*, in between. *Scylla* completed in December 1969. The Leander class formed the main part of the Fleet's frigate strength for many years, and their raised forecastles, clearly seen in this launching view, made them excellent seaboats. She visited the Far East and also took part in the Cod War of 1973, during which she was damaged by ramming. She also took part in the 1975-76 Cod War and provided hurricane relief in Cuba in 1980. She was modernised with Sea Wolf and Exocet missiles at Devonport in 1982-84. Paid off in December 1993, she was sunk as a dive site in Whitsand Bay on 27 March 2004. (*Dave Scoble Collection*)

The 3,040-ton trials and research vessel **Crystal** was named at Devonport on 20 March 1971, but launching was delayed until 22 March due to high winds. She was completed in September 1971. She was towed from Devonport on 13 December 1971 to replace the research vessels **Duchess of Argyll** and **J. Farley** at Portland. She was 413.5 feet long and had a beam of 56 feet, but her main feature was a six-storey laboratory block. She was towed to Devonport for refits in 1976 and 1981. She was sold to a Dutch firm for breaking up and towed to Rotterdam on 18 September 1992.

(*S.V. Goodman Collection*)

This view of No. 10 dock in 1959 shows the **Ark Royal** undergoing a major refit - note the catapult extension over her bow. She had been launched on 3 May 1950 by Cammell Laird, and was completed in February 1955. At 43,060-tons, she was the Royal Navy's largest aircraft carrier, and underwent several modernisations and refits at Devonport during her career. In the foreground, in No. 4 Basin, are the small Dog class tug **Alsatian** (1961), the Director class paddle tug **Director** (1956) and the water boat **Freshpond** (1945). **Ark Royal** finally paid off in 1978, and was broken up at Cairnryan in September 1980.

(*Author's Collection*)

This view from the north west corner of the North Yard of Devonport shows the misty outline of the depot ship *Forth* underneath one of the last DC electric goose-neck cranes. *Forth* was a submarine depot ship launched in 1938, and which had just returned from the Far East. She was brought alongside this berth and renamed *Defiance* on 15 February 1972 as the Fleet Maintenance Base for Devonport and as the depot ship for the Second Submarine Squadron. Meanwhile, work was started clearing the old coaling wharf in preparation for a purpose built shore maintenance base. When that opened on 21 April 1978, the *Defiance* ex *Forth* was laid up in the Hamoaze. She was towed to the breakers in the Medway in July 1985. Meanwhile, the shore base was named *Defiance* on 12 March 1981. It was absorbed into *Drake* in March 1994. In the foreground are a couple of donkey boilers, used to provide steam services for vessels alongside.

*(S.V. Goodman Collection)*

The frigates **Scarborough** (foreground) and **Tenby** (astern) are seen lying off the North Yard. In the background can be seen the Barrack's accommodation blocks. These two Type 12, Whitby class anti-submarine frigates had served in the Dartmouth Training Squadron from 1963 (**Tenby**) and 1964 (**Scarborough**), and so had been regular visitors to Devonport for many years. For this task they had extra deckhouses and boats fitted abaft their funnels. They were both proposed for sale to Pakistan in 1974, but this sale was not completed. **Scarborough** arrived at Blyth to be broken up on 31 August 1977, and **Tenby** arrived at Briton Ferry 15 days later, also to be broken up. (*S.V. Goodman Collection*)

This is a general view of the Prince of Wales Basin looking southwards towards Mount Edgcumbe and Plymouth Sound, and was taken in about 1971. The aircraft carrier **Ark Royal** lies in dry dock, with the aircraft carrier **Centaur** in the basin. **Centaur** was used as an accommodation ship for **Eagle's** refit of 1966-67, and she was then towed to Portsmouth for a similar duty there until 1970. She was then brought back to Devonport for use as an accommodation ship from 1971 until taken for breaking up in July 1972. Two tank landing ships lie on the south wall of the basin, with **Messina** outboard. These ships were used as dockyard offices and storerooms. A landing ship dock (**Fearless** or **Intrepid**) is on the sea wall, with a County class destroyer astern of her. The Basin was opened in February 1907 by the Prince of Wales, later King George V. The work had started in 1896, covering some 114 acres of reclaimed land, and included Nos. 4 and 5 Basins, graving docks and support workshops.

*(S.V. Goodman Collection)*

The cruiser **Tiger** (*inboard*) was laid down to an improved Colony class design, but completed in 1959 as a gun cruiser with automatic 6-inch and 3-inch guns. She started a conversion to a helicopter carrier in 1968 at Devonport. The after end was completely stripped and a hangar and flight deck fitted. Her sister ship, **Lion**, which was lying idle and not scheduled for conversion, was used to provide spares. During the latter stages of the refit, **Lion** was brought into the basin and berthed alongside **Tiger** to ease the transfer of any items required. **Lion** arrived at Inverkeithing to be broken up in April 1975. **Tiger's** refit completed in 1972. After ten more years' service, she was finally towed from Portsmouth for breaking up in Spain on 23 September 1986. Note the Type 15 frigate and tank landing ship ahead of the cruisers, and the second tank landing ship in dry dock.

(*Dave Scoble Collection*)

The aircraft carrier **Ark Royal** is seen here departing from No. 5 wharf. The ship's company can be seen manning the whole perimeter of her large flight deck. By this stage in her career, all of her 4.5-inch guns had been removed, and she was fitted with the latest catapult gear for launching Phantom aircraft. Over her stern can be seen a coastal survey ship. On the eastern wall of No. 4 Basin is an ocean survey ship alongside a Leander class frigate. The assault ship **Fearless** is berthed on the southern wall of the basin, with the stern door which gave access to her dock for landing craft showing clearly.

(*MoD/Crown Copyright*)

In the foreground of this photograph, taken at Wilcove (on the Cornish side of the Tamar) in about 1980, is the depot ship *Forth*, which had been used as the fleet maintenance base at Devonport under the name *Defiance* from 1972-78. She was sold and arrived on the River Medway on 25 July 1985 to be broken up. Ahead of her lie the frigates *Ulster* and *Salisbury*. *Ulster* was originally a fleet destroyer, and had been converted to a fast anti-submarine frigate in 1953. She was used as a training ship for Sea Cadets from 1977 until she was towed to Inverkeithing to be broken up in November 1980. The air direction frigate *Salisbury*, which had been built at Devonport, was used as a training ship for the training establishment **HMS Raleigh** from 1980-85, and was expended as a target in September 1985.

*(S.V. Goodman Collection)*

This aerial view shows the initial excavations in preparation for the building of the frigate complex in the North Yard. Work started in January 1973 with the digging out of the original No. 2 Basin and 5, 6 and 7 docks to provide the space for three enclosed docks. 170,000 cubic metres of material were excavated, and 30,000 cubic metres of granite demolished. 270,000 cubic metres of concrete were used in the construction together with 7,000 tonnes of reinforcement. The new docks measured 134 by 19.8 metres. The frigate *Galatea* carried out the first trial docking in March 1977. The complex was opened on 23 September 1977 by the Right Hon. Dr. David Owen, then the Foreign and Commonwealth Secretary. In the first year some 27 docking were conducted in the complex.

*(S. V. Goodman Collection)*

The fast minelayer **Manxman** was launched on 5 September 1940 and completed in June 1941 by Stephen's on the Clyde. She was armed with three twin 4-inch guns and had a speed of 40 knots to allow her to carry her load of 100 mines deep into enemy held waters. She was badly damaged when torpedoed in November 1942, repairs taking to 1945. In 1961-63 she was converted to a minesweeper headquarters ship, with reduced machinery, halving her power and limiting her speed to 26 knots. In 1969 she was attached to the Royal Naval Engineering College at Manadon (located just a mile or so from the Dockyard) for training young engineer officers. She is pictured in that role in Plymouth Sound. The doors in her stern were those used for laying mines. She was paid off in 1971, and arrived at Newport to be broken up on 6 October 1972.

*(Author's Collection)*

This view shows the Rothesay class frigate *Berwick* berthed in the Frigate Complex. *Berwick* had been launched on 15 December 1959 by Harland and Wolff, and completed in June 1961. She is seen here after her 1971 modernisation, which enabled her to operate a helicopter. She paid off on 18 October 1985, and was towed from Portsmouth to be expended as a target on 18 August 1986. All the necessary services are provided to ships in the Complex - water, electricity, sewage disposal, fire-main supplies, low-pressure air etc. The entrance can be closed with shutters to provide a dry environment in which work can be carried out regardless of the weather.

*(MoD/Crown Copyright)*

Even in peacetime, ships sometimes require repairing in the dockyards. In this instance, the Leander class frigate *Achilles* had collided with a tanker in the English Channel in thick fog in 1975. The extent of repairs required to her bows can be seen clearly in the inset view. *Achilles* was launched by Yarrow on 21 November 1968, and completed in June 1970. Just prior to the collision she had been in the Far East and had evacuated refugees from Vietnam. She joined the Dartmouth Training Squadron in 1989, and paid off in 1990. She was sold to Chile in December 1990, and renamed *Ministro Zenteno*. She sailed for Chile from Devonport onboard a ship carrier (*see page 135*). (*S.V. Goodman Collection*)

In this photograph a submarine can be seen in need of the dockyard's specialist skills! This unknown 'A' or 'T' class submarine can be seen berthed on the south wall of the non-tidal No. 2 basin in the North Yard. Substantial damage can be seen to the submarine's conning tower (fin) and periscope tubes resulting from either a collision whilst underwater or trying to pass under a low bridge. Could this be the *Andrew* after being 'caught' by the Teignmouth trawler *Emma Will* in 1973? The submarine's snort tube is in the stowed position on the casing. The retaining clamp for the snort tube (diesel engine intake/exhaust) can be seen below and to one side of the stern 'overtaking' light.    (*Dave Scoble Collection*)

The Leander class frigate **Penelope** is seen here in the Prince of Wales Basin by the cantilever crane, which was subsequently dismantled. **Penelope** was launched on 17 August 1962 by Vickers Armstrong on the Tyne, and completed in October 1963. She was used for various trials, including the Seawolf anti-aircraft missile system and also towing trials for acoustic research. For a period she was without her twin 4.5-inch gun forward. From January 1978 to January 1982 she was in Devonport Dockyard's hands for the fitting of the Exocet missile system. This photograph was taken during that refit. She took part in the Falklands War in 1982. She paid off in 1991 and was sold to Ecuador and renamed **Presidento Eloy Alfaro**. The turbine shop on the jetty by **Penelope** has now been replaced by facilities to support Trident submarine refits.

(*Dave Scoble Collection*)

This spectacular view shows the aircraft carrier *Ark Royal* testing her catapults with a dummy load. A floating crane can just be seen standing by alongside the carrier to hoist the dummy load back onto the flight deck after it has been recovered by a tug. This test was very important, especially to the pilots who were to trust their lives to the efficiency of the catapult system. A lighter note was sometimes sounded with this equipment, with the launching into space of old cars or even the odd upright piano. The need for catapults was obviated when the Navy gave up fixed wing flying, and used only helicopters, relying on the Royal Air Force to provide fighter cover.

*(Andy Endacott Collection)*

This view shows the Royal Navy's two largest aircraft carriers, the ***Eagle***, laid up, on the left, with the ***Ark Royal***, in commission, on the right, leaving harbour. ***Eagle*** had been launched on 19 March 1946, but was not completed until October 1951. Later she had been equipped with the most modern Type 984 radar, whose searchlight aerial can be seen above her bridge. She was laid up in 1972 and was towed away to be broken up in October 1978. Her sister ship, ***Ark Royal***, was not launched until 3 May 1950 and not completed until February 1955. She underwent various refits to enable her to operate the most modern aircraft. She was not left idle for long, but was towed to Cairnryan to be broken up in September 1980. In the distance can be seen the destroyer ***Bristol*** lying off Weston Mill Lake.

(*Dave Lee*)

The aircraft carrier **Eagle** is seen here on her last voyage, with Stadden Heights in the background. She was towed to Cairnryan for breaking up in October 1978. The tugs bringing her out of harbour were, on the right, the 1,036-ton, 'R' class tug **Robust**, completed in 1972. She was sold in September 1997. On **Eagle's** starboard side is her sister ship **Rollicker**, completed in 1973. She was sold to a New Zealand company in 1997 and renamed **Joseph Brown**. On **Eagle's** starboard bow is the third 'R' class tug **Roysterer**, completed in 1971 and sold in 1997. The paddle tug on **Eagle's** port side was the Director class **Faithful** of 1957, which was sunk as a target off Gibraltar in April 1983. (*Michael Lennon*)

On 4 December 1978 *Ark Royal* arrived at Devonport for the last time. She is seen here coming alongside with the crew manning the flight deck, and with their families waiting on the jetty. It took until May 1979 to complete de-storing her, and on 28 September 1980 she arrived at Cairnryan to start being broken up, less than two years after her sister *Eagle* had arrived there. One of *Ark Royal's* anchors was placed near Plymouth Hoe, and another sent to the Fleet Air Arm Museum at Yeovilton, where they remain. (*S.V. Goodman Collection*)

The inshore minesweeper *Flintham* is seen passing Mount Edgcumbe on her way up harbour with trainees embarked for initial sea experience. Launched on 10 March 1955 by J.Bolson and Son, Poole, she was placed in operational reserve from 1955-64. She then commissioned as a tender to the boys' training establishment **HMS Ganges** in Suffolk, and in 1974 transferred to Devonport to run for the training establishment **HMS Raleigh**. She was paid off in 1981 and sold in March 1983. Note the shackle and spike logo on her mast to indicate her role in seamanship training.

*(S.V. Goodman Collection)*

The River Display was always a major attraction at Plymouth Navy Days. In this scene the fast training boat *Sabre* is seen at speed passing the inshore minehunter *Aveley*, with two Lynx helicopters passing overhead. *Sabre* was launched by Vosper Thornycroft on 2 April 1970 and was powered by two Proteus gas turbines giving her a speed of 40 knots. She had two Foden engines for cruising. Unarmed, she operated out of Portland for fleet anti-fast patrol boat training. She was sold in December 1986 and became the Greek yacht *El Condor*. *Aveley* was launched on 16 February 1953 by J. Samuel White, Cowes, and was fitted with a large deckhouse aft for the use of her divers when minehunting. From 1963-80 she was a training tender for the training establishment *HMS Raleigh*. In May 1983 she was sold to the Sea Cadet Corps at Woolwich, but finally sold to Pounds at Portsmouth in November 1986 for breaking up.

*(MoD/Crown Copyright)*

The air direction frigate **Lincoln** was a sister to the Devonport built **Salisbury**, and was launched on 6 April 1959 by Fairfield, completing in July 1960. She underwent a major modernisation of her radar equipment at Devonport in 1966-68, which involved a complete renewal of her masts and after structure. The engine exhausts of these diesel-powered ships were incorporated into the mast structure. This view of her shows the extra bow and stern protection of wooden sleepers fitted at Devonport when the Icelandic gunboats started ramming Royal Naval ships in the Cod Wars. She is seen passing Mutton Cove (Devonport) on her way out of the harbour towards Plymouth Sound. **Lincoln** arrived at Inverkeithing in April 1983 to be broken up.

(*S.V. Goodman Collection*)

The logistic landing ship **Sir Galahad** is seen here sailing for the Falkland Island War on 6 April 1982. Launched by Stephen on 19 April 1968, she was taken over by the Royal Fleet Auxiliary in March 1970, having previously been operated by the B.I.S.N. Co. She had a speed of 17 knots and was capable of carrying 340 troops, and more for short periods. On this occasion she was loaded with motor transport and also three Gazelle helicopters for No. 3 Commando Brigade Air Squadron. On 24 May 1982 she was hit by a bomb in San Carlos Water. The bomb failed to explode but a fire started and she went aground. The bomb was removed and she was refloated. On 8 June she was attacked by aircraft off Fitzroy Cove and set on fire again. Five of her crew were killed and 11 were injured, and many of the troops embarked were killed or badly burnt. She had to be sunk by torpedo on 25 June 1982.

*(MoD/Crown Copyright)*

The Cunard container ship ***Atlantic Conveyor*** of 14,946 tons built in 1970, was requisitioned for service in the Falklands War on 16 April 1982. In nine days Devonport Dockyard fitted her out with a flight deck protected from the South Atlantic weather by screens and containers, allowing her to operate helicopters and Harrier 'jump jet' aircraft. She is seen here leaving the Prince of Wales Basin with the frigate ***Salisbury*** in the basin, and two Leander class frigates on the river wall. She was also carrying many tons of stores for the troops involved in the campaign. She sailed from Devonport on 25 April 1982 with Naval Party 1840 embarked. On 25 May she was hit by an Exocet missile off the Falkland Islands, and sank four days later whilst under tow.

*(Author's Collection)*

The roll-on, roll-off ferry **Contender Bezant** was another ship requisitioned for the Falklands War. She was built in Venice in 1981 and sailed from Devonport on 15 May 1982 after being loaded with stores and fitted out as an auxiliary aircraft carrier, complete with hangar, fuel stowage and with two helicopter operating decks. She carried four Chinook helicopters in her cargo. She had Naval Party 2050 embarked. She returned to the UK in August 1982, and was purchased by the Ministry of Defence two years later and renamed **RFA Argus**. She was used as an air training ship and later as a primary casualty receiving ship. The frigate **Sirius** and maintenance ship **Berry Head** can be seen in the background of this photograph.

(*Author's Collection*)

The Union Steam Ship passenger Ro-Ro vessel ***Rangatira*** of 9,387 tons, built in 1972, was requisitioned for the Falkland War in May 1982. She underwent a refit at Devonport lasting 22 days prior to sailing to Southampton to embark Royal Engineers. She was armed with four 20-mm guns, fitted with a flight deck, given extra communications equipment and extra catering facilities. She is seen here leaving 10 Dock attended by the Adept class tug ***Careful*** and Felicity class tug ***Florence***. She sailed from Southampton on 19 June with Naval Party 2070, and spent 486 days at sea. She returned to Plymouth on 18 October 1983. She was returned to her owners, and in 1987 was sold to Royal Sea Ferries Ltd., Cyprus, and renamed ***Queen M***.

*(S.V. Goodman Collection)*

The Type 22 frigate **Broadsword** is seen here returning to Devonport from the Falklands War on 23 July 1982. She had been launched by Yarrow on 12 May 1976 and completed in February 1979. She was armed with Seawolf anti-aircraft missiles and Exocet missile launchers forward, and also carried a helicopter. In March 1982 she was on passage to the Far East, but was diverted to escort the aircraft carrier **Hermes** to the South Atlantic. On 25 May she was with the destroyer **Coventry**, when both ships came under attack by Argentine aircraft. The destroyer was sunk, and **Broadsword** hit by a bomb, which failed to explode but wrecked her helicopter. On 31 March 1995 she was sold to Brazil and renamed **Greenhalgh**.

*(Author's Collection)*

The 2,750-ton Type 21 frigate *Arrow* is seen here returning to Devonport after the Falklands War on 7 July 1982, having been greeted by a display from the Red Arrows. Her 4.5-inch gun, seen on her forecastle, had been put to good use during the conflict. She had been present when the destroyer *Sheffield* had been hit, and had stood by her providing assistance in fire-fighting and rescuing the crew. She had been launched on 5 February 1974 by Yarrow and completed in May 1976. Powered by gas turbines, she had a speed of over 31 knots, and also had a remarkably good acceleration. In March 1994 she was sold to Pakistan and renamed *Khaibur*. *(Author's Collection)*

The **Forth** was one of two specially built submarine depot ships. She was launched on 11 August 1938 on the Clyde, and was originally armed with four twin 4.5-inch guns and two quadruple 2-pounders. She served the Second Submarine Flotilla from 1939-41, and then the Third Submarine Flotilla. Post war she was disarmed and fitted with extra workshops and accommodation to handle modern submarines. After a spell in Malta and the Far East she returned to Devonport. In February 1972 she was brought alongside 9 Wharf at Devonport and renamed **Defiance**. She was then used as the Fleet Maintenance Base and also depot ship for the Second Submarine Squadron. Over the following years the Submarine Squadron grew in size and new nuclear submarines of the 'S' class were completed and joined it. She paid off in April 1978, when new shore offices and workshops had been completed. After a short period lying alongside providing temporary berthing facilities, she was laid up in the Hamoaze. In July 1985 she was towed to the Medway to be broken up. *(T. Ferrers-Walker Collection)*

The Leander class frigate **Scylla** was launched at Devonport on 8 August 1968, and completed in December 1969. On completion she assisted with acoustic trials by towing her sister ship **Penelope** at speeds up to 23 knots. She visited the Far East and took part in the 1973 Cod War off Iceland, where she was in collision with the Icelandic gunboat **Aegir**. In 1974 she visited Australia and in 1975-76 took part in more Cod War patrols. From November 1980 to December 1984 she was modernised at Devonport. As seen in this photograph taken at the end of her refit, she then had a Sea Wolf missile system and Exocet missile launchers fitted forward in place of her 4.5-inch turret, and her masts, funnel and after structure had been modified to save weight. She paid off on 14 December 1993 after a voyage through the Panama Canal. She was sunk as a dive-site in Whitsand Bay on 27 March 2004.    (*S.V. Goodman Collection*)

In this view of the Prince of Wales Basin, the diesel powered submarine **Opportune** lies nearest the camera. Launched on 14 February 1964 by Scotts, these 'O' class submarines were a development of the Porpoise class and proved very successful. Submarines of this type served in the Australian, Canadian, Brazilian and Chilean Navies. Of 1,610 tons, she was originally armed with eight torpedo tubes, but two were later removed. She was laid up in 1993 and sold to Pounds of Portsmouth in 1996 to be broken up. In the background lies the destroyer **Liverpool**. She had been launched by Cammell Laird on 25 September 1980 and completed in 1982. She was the only Devonport based Type 42 destroyer. The Royal Naval Barracks can be seen in the background.

*(S.V. Goodman Collection)*

The Mark 8 4.5-inch gun of the Type 21 frigate ***Ambuscade*** is seen here being replaced by a complete new gun on 5 March 1985, whilst the ship lies in the Frigate Complex on 5 March 1985. The ***Ambuscade*** had been launched on 18 January 1973 by Yarrow and completed in September 1975. She took part in the Falklands War in 1982, where her gun proved invaluable for shore bombardment. Designed by Vosper Thornycroft, these frigates carried a helicopter, and were very manoeuvrable. Their hulls were strengthened in the mid-1980s. ***Ambuscade*** paid off in May 1993, was sold to Pakistan and renamed ***Tariq*** on 28 July 1993.

*(S. V. Goodman Collection)*

This scene shows the ever-popular Plymouth Navy Days. Originally instigated between the wars to boost the King George V Fund for Sailors when naval pay was appallingly low. It used to be held for a whole week. Post World War Two it was held twice a year over Bank holiday weekends. Later it reduced to once a year, and then to every other year. Here, the County class guided missile destroyer *Fife* is the inboard ship on the river wall, with an Ikara fitted Leander class frigate outboard of her. Astern lie two Type 22 frigates. *Fife* was launched on 9 March 1964 by Fairfield. She suffered a major fire in the Mediterranean in November 1970. She was part of the Dartmouth Training Squadron from 1982-87 and was sold to Chile in 1987 and renamed **Blanco Encalada**. She was converted to a helicopter carrier in 1994 and deleted in 2003. (*S.V. Goodman Collection*)

The wreck of the old submarine *Holland 01* was discovered off Plymouth in 1982. It was recovered in December 1982, and is seen here in dry dock prior to being transported to the Submarine Museum at Gosport. *Holland 01* had been launched on 2 October 1901 by Vickers and Sons, and was completed in February 1903. Of 120 tons, she had one torpedo tube and a crew of seven. She was the Royal Navy's first submarine, and was named after her designer A.P. Holland. She had a single hull with an internal ballast tank, and her hull shape had a very modern look. She had been sold on 7 October 1913 and was lost off the Eddystone Light while being towed to Briton Ferry to be broken up. She was recovered by ***RMAS Pintail*** and the hull carefully preserved in the Dockyard to prevent further deterioration.

(*J. Sharp*)

The River Class fleet minesweeper *Carron* is seen here off the southern part of the South Yard by the oldest building slips of the original dockyard. Of 890 tons at full load, she was launched by Richards at Great Yarmouth on 23 September 1983, and was commissioned for service with the Severn Division of the Royal Naval Reserve from September 1984. She had twin funnels and rear facing windows in her bridge to provide good visibility aft for minesweeping. These ships had steel hulls as they were designed to operate in deep water clear of influence mines. She paid off in April 1993. On 3 September 1994 she was renamed *Shaikat* on transfer to the Bangladesh Navy.

*(Dave Scoble)*

The Royal Fleet Auxiliary *Argus* was originally the Ro-Ro- ferry **Contender Bezant**. She was built in Venice in 1981, and requisitioned for the Falklands War in 1982. She was purchased by the Ministry of Defence in March 1984, and converted to an air training ship by Harland and Wolff. She was named *Argus* on 25 March 1987. She displaces 28,081 tons and has a speed of 18 knots. In 1990 she was converted to be a primary casualty receiving ship with 100 hospital beds and surgical capability. She served in the 1991 Kuwait operation. She is seen here passing the Royal William Yard on her way out of harbour towards Plymouth Sound.

*(Devonport Management Limited)*

The 'S' class submarine *Sovereign* is seen here docking in the new Submarine Refit Complex, which had been opened by HRH Prince Charles in May 1980. The work to build the Complex had taken 7 years, and cost £60 million, providing two dry docks, a wet berth and an 80-tonne crane. *Sovereign* was launched on 17 February 1973 at Barrow, and completed in February 1974. She displaces 4,200 tons and is armed with five torpedo tubes. Her reactor core was replaced in 1993-95, and she is scheduled to pay off finally in 2006.    (*S.V. Goodman Collection*)

The nuclear submarine *Superb* is seen here in September 1985 conducting a basin dive as part of the underwater trials which took place four weeks before the completion of her refit at Devonport.  She had been launched by Vickers on 30 November 1974, and completed in November 1976.  In December 2001 she returned to the UK flying a Jolly Roger after anti-terrorist operations in the Middle East, during which she covered 20,000 miles and operated in the Indian Ocean.  She is scheduled to pay off for the last time in 2006.

*(S.V. Goodman Collection)*

The Leander classs frigate **Penelope** is seen here in No. 9 Dock, with a view beyond her of the married quarters estate which has replaced the old **Impregnable** training establishment. This view shows the frigate after her 1978-82 modernisation, carried out at Devonport, when Exocet and Seacat missiles were fitted. Her single 40-mm guns mounted each side of her bridge are protected by canvas covers. The timber supports to retain the docked ship in position are visible here, as is the network of pipes and cables supplying power, air and water to the ship. No. 9 dock has since been modernised and is now used for Vanguard class Trident submarine refits.     (*Dave Scoble Collection*)

The aircraft carrier **Invincible** is seen here entering harbour, whilst the maintenance ship **Berry Head** is being towed out by the 'R' class tug **Robust**. **Berry Head**, built in 1944 at Vancouver, had been used as an accommodation ship in the yard from 1976-88. She was then taken to Portsmouth to de-equip prior to being sold to Turkey for breaking up in March 1990. **Invincible** was launched by Vickers at Barrow on 3 May 1977 and completed in March 1980. She took part in the Falklands War of 1982 and underwent a major refit at Devonport from 1986-88, during which her flight deck, communications and AA defences were all upgraded.

*(Dave Scoble Collection)*

The aircraft carrier ***Illustrious*** is seen here entering the River Tamar escorted by the 'R' class tug ***Rollicker*** and Adept class tugs ***Careful*** and ***Faithful***. ***Illustrious*** was launched on 1 December 1978 by Swan Hunter. Her completion was brought forward because of the Falklands War, and she commissioned at sea in June 1982. After several years being laid up at Portsmouth, ***Illustrious*** arrived in Devonport in 1991 to start a major refit during which her flight deck was extended, and the angle of her ramp increased. A new main mast was also fitted. The refit took 3 years. Beyond her can be seen the Royal William Yard and Drake's Island, with Stadden Heights in the distance.

(*Dave Scoble Collection*)

This general view of the Prince of Wales Basin was probably taken in 1994. Nearest the camera is the air training ship **RFA Argus**. Beyond her is the aircraft carrier **Illustrious**, being warped out of No. 9 Dock on completion of her three-year £100 million refit. The 31,565-ton replenishment ship **RFA Fort George** is in the north-east corner of the basin. A group of 5 dockyard riggers can be seen manning the warping capstan on the edge of the basin. The wire from the capstan can be seen leading up to the starboard bow of **Illustrious**. Other wires from her bow and stern would be leading to other capstans sited round the basin. This precise manoeuvre has always to be conducted in very still conditions by skilled men. The Admiralty pilot can be seen on the carrier's flying bridge. The large crane in the background is used to refuel nuclear submarines in 11 and 12 docks.

*(Dave Scoble Collection)*

Nearest to the camera in this view of Plymouth Sound is the 1,915-ton survey ship *Hecla*. She was launched on 21 December 1964 by Yarrow at Blythwood. During the Falklands War she was employed as a hospital ship. In 1991 she took part in operations off Kuwait supporting mine-countermeasures forces. She was sold to Ross Marine in March 1997 and renamed *Bligh*. She was broken up in 2004. The smaller coastal survey vessel on her way out to sea is the 1,050-ton *Bulldog*, launched by Brooke Marine on 12 July 1967. She was sold in August 2001 for conversion to a yacht, but was destroyed by fire in New Zealand in May 2004. From 1998 Survey ships discarded their traditional white paint in favour of normal warship grey. Devonport is not only the base for the Navy's Hydrographic Service, but is also home to the Hydrographic School.

(*MoD/Crown Copyright*)

A stranger to Devonport was the Royal Yacht **Britannia**. The 3,990-ton yacht was launched on 16 April 1953 on the Clyde, and, at 412.2 feet overall was 40 feet longer than a Leander class frigate, though the later Type 22 frigates were 18 feet longer. Extra care was required to avoid scraping the gleaming paintwork on the hull of the **Britannia** as she slipped gently into the dock for maintenance. **Britannia** was paid off in December 1997, and arrived at Leith on 5 May 1998 for use as a exhibition ship. The modern construction of the new Frigate Complex contrasts with the old 19th Century buildings which remain beside it.

*(MoD/Crown Copyright)*

The nuclear powered submarine *Trafalgar* is seen here being brought into a basin by the small, powerful and manoeuvrable Dog class tugs *Mastiff* and *Corgi*, assisted by the smaller Felecity class tug *Frances*. *Trafalgar* was launched on 1 July 1981 by Vickers at Barrow, and completed in May 1983. Armed with 5 torpedo tubes, she test fired the Tomahawk missile in 2001. She was the first British submarine to circumnavigate the World via the Panama and Suez Canals. The Trafalgar class submarines form the main part of the Fleet's submarine force. She is scheduled to pay off in 2008.

*(Dave Scoble Collection)*

The 2,750-ton type 21 frigate *Ambuscade* is seen here in the Frigate Complex. She was launched on 18 January 1973 by Yarrow and completed in 1975. She took part in the Falklands War in 1982 and continued in service for a further 11 years, until paying off in May 1993. She was then sold to Pakistan and renamed TARIQ in July 1993. The doors which close to protect the dock from the weather can be seen astern of *Ambuscade*. Each door comprises four leaves 26 by 10 metres. Work on the Complex started in January 1973 and involved excavation work as well the construction of the (then) unique covered buildings together with pumping systems. The steel structure of the cover won a 1976 Design Award of the European Convention for Constructional Steelwork.

*(S.V. Goodman Collection)*

The Leander class frigate **Achilles** was launched by Yarrow on 21 November 1968.  She was handed over to the Royal Navy at Devonport in November 1970.  In 1974-75 she was part of a Task Group that deployed to the Indian Ocean, Far East and South America.  Being one of the later vessels of her class completed, she was never modernised with Exocet missiles, but retained her twin 4.5-inch gun.  She was sold to Chile in December 1990, and renamed **Ministro Zenteno**.  She was transported to Chile from Devonport onboard the heavy lift vessel **Super Servant 4**, which can be seen here carrying the frigate 'piggy-back' fashion, as she sails from Plymouth on 1 December 1990.  *(Dave Scoble Collection)*

The Fleet tender **Manly**, together with her sisters **Mentor** and **Milbrook**, was used by **HMS Raleigh** to provide initial sea experience for newly entered ratings. She was launched by Dunstan on 23 July 1981, and displaced 143 tons. She was 80 feet long. She was sold to Pounds of Portsmouth in February 1992 for further service. Beyond her can be seen the 'R' class tug **Robust**. Built in 1972 by C.D. Holmes and designed for ocean towing, she had twin controllable pitch propellers and twin rudders making her very manoeuvrable. She was sold in September 1997 to International Ship Repair and Marine Services of Tampa, Florida.

*(MoD/Crown Copyright)*

The Type 42 destroyer **Liverpool** is seen here passing Mount Edgcumbe on her way up harbour. She had been launched on 25 September 1980 by Cammell Laird, and was accepted on 12 May 1982. She was the last of the first group of Type 42s, the subsequent four of the class being longer. She was the only Devonport based vessel of her type. These ships carry individual ship name symbols on their funnels. They are handsome, well balanced ships, but are already being phased out, albeit after much arduous service. She carried out Gulf Patrols and in September 2002 fired the first salvo of Sea Dart missiles in a decade, achieving a direct hit on a sea-skimming target.

*(MoD/Crown Copyright)*

The Trafalgar class submarine **Torbay** is seen here being manoeuvred by the Dog class tugs **Corgi** and **Saluki**. Beyond, alongside the river wall, lies the Type 22 frigate **Beaver**. This scene demonstrates the careful handling required to move ships and submarines around the dockyard, and why strong winds can delay operations. **Torbay** was launched on 8 March 1985 by Vickers and completed in February 1987. She has the quieter pump jet propulsion, unlike **Trafalgar**, which has a seven bladed propeller. **Torbay** is scheduled to serve in the fleet to 2021.

*(Dave Scoble Collection)*

The Type 21 frigate *Arrow* is seen here at the ever-popular Navy Days, with her decks crowded with visitors all watching a Wessex helicopter taking part in the River Display. Despite the crowds, the handsome lines of these frigates are clearly visible. *Arrow* was launched on 5 February 1974 by Yarrow, and completed in May 1976. She attended the Queen's Jubilee Review of the Fleet in June 1977. She was refitted in 1979, and took part in the Falklands War in 1982, when two of her sister ships, *Ardent* and *Antelope* were lost. Her 4.5-inch gun seen here was put to good effect during bombardments. On 1 March 1994 she was handed over to the Pakistan Navy at Devonport and renamed *Khaibur*.

(*S.V. Goodman Collection*)

The 7,500-ton nuclear powered submarine **Repulse** is photographed here secured to Charlie Buoy in Plymouth Sound, with Mount Edgcumbe country park in the background. Her ship's company are fallen in on the casing, ready for her to proceed up river to the naval base. This is thought to be the first and only occasion that the nuclear ballistic armed submarine visited Devonport. She was one of four Resolution class submarines completed between 1967-69, and were all based at Faslane in Scotland. Until superseded by the SSBNs of the Vanguard class, these four vessels had the responsibility of providing the Nation's nuclear deterrent for a period of 28 years. **Repulse** was decommissioned in August 1996 after 59 patrols, and is now laid up at Rosyth.

(*Dave Scoble Collection*)

The Type 42 destroyer *Nottingham* is seen here emerging from the Frigate Complex. Her refit is nearly over, but she still has scaffolding around her mainmast, and covers over much of her equipment. The large steel shutters at the entrances can be seen raised to permit her passage, with the shutters for the other two docks still closed. *Nottingham* was launched by Vospers on 18 February 1980, and arrived at Devonport on 15 September 1982 under the Red Ensign, in preparation for her acceptance in December. These ships are armed with a 4.5-inch gun and Seadart missile system forward, and carry a helicopter aft. They have gas turbine engines for both high speed and cruising. *Nottingham* grounded off Lord Howe Island, off Australia, in July 2002, but has since been repaired and rejoined the Fleet.

(*MoD/Crown Copyright*)

This aerial view shows the Leander class frigate *Ariadne* in dry dock (centre). The other docks are also in use, with the Reasearch barge *Crystal* and two Iranian Mk. 5 frigates *Saam* (renamed *Alvand*) and *Zaal* (renamed *Alborz*). Beyond, the Prince of Wales Basin, lie a landing ship (tank) and another Leander class frigate. *Ariadne* was the last of the 26 Leander class built for the Royal Navy. She was launched on 10 September 1971 by Yarrow, and completed in June 1972. In 1981 in the West Indies her company helped fight a fire in a power station in Bequia in the Grenadines. In 1991 she joined the Dartmouth Training Squadron and just before paying off in April 1992 carried out the last Royal Naval firing of a twin 4.5-inch gun. In May 1992 she was sold to Chile and renamed *General Baquedano*.

(*S.V. Goodman Collection*)

This general view of the north end of the North Yard shows the massive Submarine Refit Complex, with its two dry docks and 80-tonne crane. In this instance one dock is dry, and the other filled with water. Work started on the complex in 1973, and it was opened in May 1980 by HRH The Prince of Wales, appropriate as it lies in the basin opened in February 1907 by the then Prince of Wales (later King George V). Beyond the Submarine Complex can be seen the Fleet Maintenance Base and Headquarters of the Second Submarine Squadron. Along the Weston Mill Lake Jetty (10-13 wharves) lie four Leander class and one Rothesay class frigates. Across the lake lie the old jetty and rail line to the RN Armament Depot at Bull Point, now replaced by the Weston Mill Lake Jetty (14-16 wharves)

(*MoD/Crown Copyright*)

The Helicopter Assault Ship *Ocean* was launched on the Clyde on 11 October 1995 and completed at Barrow. She was commissioned at Devonport on 30 September 1998. She became fully operational in March 1999. She is the first RN such ship specifically designed for her task. She is diesel powered with a speed of 19 knots. She carries four LCVPs and two hovercraft for landing troops and has 12 Sea King and six Lynx or Gazelle helicopters. She can carry 500 troops and 40 vehicles, and can carry an extra 303 troops in overload conditions. In 1998 she provided aid in the wake of Hurricane Mitch in Central America, and has also operated off West Africa, in Afghan operations and in the Indian Ocean. She is seen here approaching Weston Mill Lake Jetty.

(*Stuart Miller*)

The *Albion* is the first of two Landing Platform Docks built to replace the *Fearless* and *Intrepid*. She was launched by Princess Anne on 9 March 2001 at Barrow, and was commissioned at Devonport on 19 June 2003. She operates 4 utility landing craft and 4 smaller LCVP and has can operate 3 Merlin helicopters. She can also operate the larger Chinook helicopter. She has a capacity of 305 troops in normal operations. Her diesel engines give her a speed of 20 knots. In this photo she is seen in the River Tamar operating both helicopters and landing craft, with her stern access under water to permit landing craft to operate from her covered dock.

*(Nick Newns)*

The Ballistic Missile submarine **Vanguard** is seen arriving at Devonport in 2002 for the first Trident submarine refit. The facilities at the dockyard were extensively modernised to allow the refitting of these 16,000 leviathans. **Vanguard** was launched on 4 March 1992 and was acceptedin September 1993. In April 1994 she carried out her first Trident firings off America and carried out her first detterent patrol in late 1995. There are four vessels in the class which replaced the Polaris armed Resolution class submarines which had maintained the deterrent role for thirty years.

*(Chris Rogers)*

# Index